DISCARDED

Sagebrush, Buttes and Buffalo

Williston, Dickinson and the Badlands

Volume Four
North Dakota Centennial Series

Published by
The Dakota Graphic Society
Fargo, North Dakota

Text: Nancy Edmonds Hanson
Photographs: Sheldon Green
Russ Hanson
Production: Leonard Roehrich
Historical photographs: State Historical Society
of North Dakota.
Printer: Knight Printing Company, Fargo.

Dakota Graphic Society
Box 9199
Fargo, North Dakota 58109

CONTENTS

299607

BAD COUNTRY TO CROSS

Dusk is the cool and vivid soul of the badlands summer.

Long shadows turn to inky blue as the sun slips toward the western horizon. The landscape — nearly two-dimensional in the scorching midday glare — stands out in sharp relief. As the ancient whistle of the wind is gentled by nightfall, other sounds are raised against the hush.

Birds trill their evening songs against the sluggish murmur of the Little Missouri River. Cottonwood leaves rustle in the breeze that's never still. In the afterglow of day, insects chirp and crackle.

Hooves of buffalo and deer click dully against the crusty clay and scoria scattered underfoot. They browse on the margin of thickets of willow and on the plots of hardy grasses marked by intersections in the deeply-sculpted landscape. Wild horses toss their manes in silhouette against the sunset.

Daylight's final glow flashes against the highest buttes, plating them with gold. Silvery junipers lean forward from clefts in the banded rock. At the base of slumping cliffs, the evening-star lily opens its moon-colored blossoms to the night. Shadows turn to basalt and the sky deepens to sapphire.

Their twisted magic has stretched across a thousand years. The badlands are alive. The spirits claim them.

Not spirits, but the practical minds of travelers gave the badlands their name. The restless Sioux called them *mako shika*, or "land bad" . . . a barrier to their buffalo hunts on horseback across the open plain.

French trappers and traders drawn to the Upper Missouri for its furs used melodious words to express the same idea: *les mauvaises terres a traverser*, "bad lands to cross."

But it was left to General Alfred Sully to introduce the concept to America. Jouncing along in an Army wagon as his troops pursued Sioux warriors, bad-tempered and sick in the searing August heat, he christened this country "badlands" — and meant it. Then he pronounced the undoubtedly heartfelt verdict that has echoed down the years: "Hell with the fires out."

Modern geologists tell a tale of earthly forces carving out the land of the Little Missouri. They speak of ancient seas and swamps, of timeless rivers, of succeeding layers of silt and bone fires in the bowels of the earth. They condense the drama in the measured words of science, and credit this creation to water and wind and fire.

Sioux storytellers told it differently. Their account of the badlands' birth was recounted in a 1938 guidebook prepared by the Federal Writers Project:

Once the badlands were a fertile plain, thick with buffalo grown fat on its rich grasses. It was a place of harmony where, each autumn, the tribes gathered to hunt and trade and hold friendly councils in the shade along the river. Though they might be hostile elsewhere, here they met in peace.

No story of Eden is without serpents. In Sioux legend, trouble came from the west. A fierce mountain tribe rode down to claim the hunters' paradise, driving the plains people out. They tried to reclaim it, but failed. Finally they met in a great council to fast and pray to the Great Spirit.

After many days without an answer, they had begun to despair . . . when suddenly a great tremor seized the earth, the sky grew black as night, and lightning burned jagged through the gloom. Fires began to flame and sizzle underfoot, and the earth tossed and pitched like the waves of the sea. The invaders sank beneath its smoking, roiling surface along with the streams, the trees and all that lived there. Then, just as abruptly as it had begun, the terror ended, leaving th eplain in grotesque disarray.

And so the Great Spirit destroyed the prize that had stirred up strife among his children, and the badlands were born.

As they did in Sioux legend, the badlands still loom large in the minds of modern North Dakotans and their visitors. They dominate accounts far out of proportion to the acreage they occupy — only a few percentage points of the state's land — and farther still beyond their residents' numbers.

Badlands country was long among the remotest and least populated regions of modern America, excluding only Alaska. Until a contingent of soldiers arrived to protect construction gangs building Northern Pacific Railroad, few but Indians and trappers and the troops of Sully and Custer had witnessed firsthand the moods and challenges of the twisted landscape's glory.

Ever intent on promoting rail travel to the midcontinental wilderness it crossed, the Northern Pacific Railroad seized on the bountiful game as a way to build traffic. Its publicists presaged modern advertising's gift for euphemism by not only extolling the badlands' virtues but trying to un-Sully their threatening name; in railroad nomenclature, the region was persistently called Pyramid Park. And thus was born the badlands' first bona fide industry, tourism.

Prompted by N.P. advertising, easterners and noble European sportsmen discovered that bison, bighorn sheep, white-tail and mule deer, pronghorn antelope and grizzlies could indeed be bagged amidst the badlands' rustic splendor. Some recognized the grazing value of this last stretch of virgin prairie, and thus was born the second industry. Vacationing sportsmen with names like Eaton and Huidekoper returned to established ranches at the badlands' heart. Texas cowboys urged enormous herds of longhorns northward to graze on blue grama and buffalo grass.

The decade of the 1880s witnessed the arrival of two men in particular who left long shadows across the Little Missouri. The Marquis de Mores brought not only dreams of a cattle empire, but plans for vertically-integrated enterprises to carry his beef all the way from calving season to the tables of urban housewives.

Scrawny, bespectacled Theodore Roosevelt came to hunt and build up his health, and remained to learn lessons that followed him to the presidency. His love affair with the incongruously fragile natural balance of the badlands helped spawn his conservationist ethic and, indirectly, creation of a system of national parks. years later, it would be memorialized where it all began in Theodore Roosevelt National Park.

Not all of western North Dakota is badlands. Yet the spirit of the real Old West that was planted there took root through a much broader, butte-strewn territory distinctly apart from the rest of the state.

Cattle continue to graze on the sun-colored grasses of the west, dotting arid pastures punctuated by the flat-topped, steep-sided hills called buttes. Shells of prehistoric marine creatures can still be spotted on their broad summits, reminders of the humid tropics that built them with layer upon layer of clay and silt in the eons of prehistory.

While cattle are common, people are a rarity. That suggests the source of the remarkable spirit that's as natural to western North Dakota as January chinooks and August droughts. Some of the friendliest strangers on earth greet visitors here with a warmth and hospitality that stand out even in a state known for the quality of its welcome.

History has taught them tough lessons. Between the weather, the grasshoppers, the economy and the beef market, western North Dakotans might have thought they'd heard them all until the decades of the 1970s and 1980s. Then, as the worldwide oil cartel drove prices toward the heavens, the petroleum industry turned in earnest to the resources deep underfoot in the Williston Basin. Western Dakota learned to handle the pressures of an economic boom . . . only to be faced with the flip side a few short years later in a hope-crushing bust.

Today oil wells still bob like comical grasshoppers along red-dust trails built with scoria, the brick-like byproduct of underground fires baking native clay. But drillers' derricks — once as common here as grain elevators in the small-grain-farming east — have become rare as the fervid wildcatting of Oil Crisis days has given way to lower gasoline prices. The nation views North Dakota's great deep reserves with less urgency these days.

The buffalo are gone . . . gone with the great historic ranches and the fevered fortune-seekers of the great oil boom. But western Dakota remains a region set apart both by history and topographics. The sagebrush, the buttes, the badlands remain — a treasure from a time before time.

Western North Dakota's wide vistas take your breath away. The wind is their constant companion. Harnessing its power was often homesteaders' first accomplishment, permitting them to draw water for their livestock and even generate electricity to light up their new homes. The badlands' tousled topography (right) dominates the Fort Berthold Reservation east of Mandaree.

"Rough country to cross" . . . and more so in winter. Sudden storms can close badlands roads, sometimes for weeks on end. Intent on choosing a name implying dependability (above), the Chrysler Corporation christened their new truck the Dodge Dakota. The company introduced the model to automotive writers in 1986 with a rally through the badlands, choosing winding scoria roads and rough country to demonstrate how the Dakota lived up to its name.

Fertile wheat farms at the badlands' edge provide a counterpoint to rough country just to the south and to the north (above) near Watford City. Regent (right) settles down amid strip-farmed grain fields in North Dakota's southwest corner.

For centuries the badlands' only visitors were buffalo and the Indian hunters who followed their annual migrations. Today, the buffalo — once nearly extinct — again roam the wide open spaces of North Dakota, thanks to a major conservation and restocking program. Mule deer also thrive in the sheltered draws and valleys between the buttes.

The Little Missouri River has relentlessly sculpted the badlands. Cutting through clay and sand, it takes on the consistency of a chocolate milkshake. South of New Town it dumps its thick waters into Lake Sakakawea, itself a dammed creation of the mighty Missouri. The lake is becoming a recreational mecca, with houseboats regularly cruising its waters from a sheltered marina at New Town.

Highway 22 at the badlands' north rim is one of the most scenic drives in the Great Plains. Skimming past the Killdeer Mountains to New Town, it crosses open range to reveal some of the most spectacular vistas in the west. The road meets Four Bears Bridge at New Town, named for a revered chief of the Three Affiliated Tribes. Parts of the bridge were brought upstream by barge from the reservation village of Elbowoods, now inundated by Lake Sakakawea.

Wild horses wade across the Little Missouri River north of Medora. Only petrified stumps (above) remain of the massive ancient forests that blanketed western North Dakota in a warmer and more humid time. Some experts claim these large petrified stumps near Keene were once sequoias.

Water, Wind and Fire

The planet Earth is seldom so alive as in the badlands.

It radiates quiet patience across most of North Dakota. The flat Red River Valley has an unearthly calm — a serene canvas that welcomes the colorful pigments lent by farming's seasons. The rolling drift prairie expresses unexpected humor: River valleys take travelers by surprise among the chuckling swells, and migrating flocks of ducks and geese respond with ghostly laughter.

West of the Missouri River, the ground takes on a tougher posture as it rises toward the west. But only in the badlands does the earth reveal the secrets of its past with a power that takes the human breath away.

North Dakota's badlands are a natural work in progress. The soil that seems so steady underfoot begins to shift and shatter. The natural elements that shaped this unfinished masterpiece — water, wind and fire — are still carving and chiseling and baking the clay. What's here today will ever so subtly change before tomorrow.

Walk in Theodore Roosevelt National Park, and feel the sting of fresh-carved sand against your cheeks: The westerly wind is whistling as it works.

Spot gnarled junipers and clumps of brush growing from the face of sheered-off cliffs. Their roots have turned a toe-hold into a network of hairline cracks, persistent proof that someday solid-looking rock will crumble.

Kick the brick-red rubble that lines the hiking path, and think of age-old kilns that once baked bricks beneath your feet. Lightning and prairie fires supplied the sparks that kindled sooty beds of lignite. The rusty rock called scoria is a reminder of subterranean fires — some inexpressably ancient, others smoldering still.

And think of water. Here, where snow and rain yield little more than an inch of moisture per month, the signature of ancient seas is an oddity. Yet salty lakes and humid swamps did leave their legacy beneath this dust-dry land across a hundred million years.

When the Little Missouri River runs high with clean, fresh run-off in the spring, it hints of its dynamic past. Its churning currents eat away at banks and wiry meadows along its course, digesting their clays and rearranging the murky load along its route — a riverbed as twisted as unraveled knitting.

Summer thunderstorms, too, testify to the power of an ageless torrent. Badlands gullies erupt with the waters of flash floods. Cedars and willows clinging to their slopes are torn and carried with the surge. The frenzy slashes at the feet of eroding cliffs, sculpting an ever-changing boundary even as the rainfall is finally swallowed by the land.

Of course, water and wind are no strangers to the rest the globe. Volcanoes erupt. Earthquakes open chasms in solid land. Yet the fact that they make headlines underscores our faith that nature's caprices are exceptions . . . that its drama is in the past. We regard the earth as a steady, stable stage for events of our own making.

But in the badlands, as in other raw young landscapes, tell-tale signs of the tumult are disquietingly clear.

This is the way the earth was born, wracked by forces that melt stone, that turn sea to land and land to sea again. This is the way the earth lives on — by consuming itself and reshaping its destiny.

North Dakota's badlands aren't a singular sort of landscape. Other weathered, sculpted stretches of naked clay and shale offer evidence of similar works in progress, including Badlands National Monument in South

Dakota and corresponding bits of Wyoming and Montana.

But North Dakota's are set apart for the size of the land they dominate (nearly two hundred miles in length and forty wide) and for their palette of colors. Every shade of dun and cream and grey are represented in their banded buttes, along with reds from deep brick to salmon. Set off by an infinite range of greens, they fade in the heat of the day only to reemerge when splashed with a sudden shower.

The spartan plants that keep their balance in the badlands' extremes of heat and cold, driness and drenching, are ironic successors to the flora of the region's past. Dense luxurious shoreline ferns flourished half a billion years ago. They laid layers of rank mulch upon the deep grey slate. Buried with silt carried by prehistoric rivers, then compressed beneath the weight of time, they turned to beds of soft lignite coal — the streaky licorice-colored stripes apparent in many outcroppings.

A quarter-billion years ago, the humid swamps returned. Dinosaurs laid claim to the land, lumbering across the steamy landscape to munch on near-tropical trees and plants and each other. Some of the ancient reptiles' bones have been uncovered here, though their past dominions is far more evident in South Dakota. The petroleum deposits of the Williston Basin (underlying most of western North Dakota and adjoining states) date back to their times.

Reminders of the region's life hundreds of millions of years ago are occasionally spotted by sharp eyes. Fossils bearing the outlines of ancient marine creatures top many buttes, themselves protected by hard rock "caps" from the erosion that whittled away the surrounding landscape.

Most familiar are the fossilized trees of the so-called petrified forests. Engulfed by volcanic ash as the Rockies were being created, then soaked with mineral-rich water,

their stumps and trunks were slowly turned to stone and left as monuments.

Far more recently, uncounted numbers of North America's proudest mammals roamed the convoluted reaches of these badlands. Hunters decimated their numbers in the nineteenth century — one of the many tragedies of the taming of the West.

Today many species are back, thanks to the conservation movement set in motion by Theodore Roosevelt three-quarters of a century ago. More than five hundred bison roam the two units of Theodore Roosevelt National Park — a hardy remnant of the billion beasts that once roamed the Great Plains.

Deer abound in the shelter at the foot of the park's twisted buttes, and pronghorn antelope sometimes skim the horizon. Bighorn sheep have been reintroduced after the native species was extinguished by early sportsmen. They live out their nimble lives unseen by all but a handful of men and women familiar with the national park's back country. Elk

were brought back to the badlands in only a few years ago.

Two living reminders of more recent history roam the parklands — wild horses and Texas longhorn cattle. Some believe the herd of dozens of wild horses are the descendants of Sitting Bull's war ponies. The longhorns owe their enviable nomadic existence to the National Park Service, which manages their numbers in tribute to the hardy dogies that cowboys drove north to graze on virgin badlands grasses a century ago.

The hills and valleys are alive with smaller wildlife as well. Tens of thousands of sociable prairie dogs claim sanctuary in the park, building their cities of underground dens unhindered by ranchers who consider them a nuisance. They play a part in the survival of more bloodthirsty beasts as well — coyotes, badgers, foxes, hawks and bald eagles. All told, close to two hundred species of birds live in the badlands on and off during the year, along with another singular resident, the prairie rattlesnake.

Human nature once threatened to be the badlands downfall, as its native game was hunted to the brink of extinction and its grasses were overgrazed by too many ravenous cattle. It's interesting, then, to note that only human management has saved North Dakota's tracts of badlands and upland prairie from destruction.

Thanks to National Park Service management and the work of individual ranchers throughout the region, the badlands have been allowed to regain their balance.

The river still runs, and countless creeks still swell with sudden downpours. The wind still blows. Fires still burn in lignite beds beneath the earth, kindled by lightning strikes and prairies fires that blacken and renew the landscape.

But when tricks of temperature obscure the valleys with fog on summer mornings, and when golden groves of cottonwoods preside beneath deep blue skies in autumn, the badlands seem at peace with the boiling forces that formed them.

(Overleaf, page 20) Whittled away by wind and water, Wind Canyon provides one of the premiere vistas of the south unit of Theodore Roosevelt National Park. South of Medora (page 21) the Little Missouri uncovers evidence of the fire that also sculpted the badlands in a large scoria sandbar. Together, the elements of wind, water and fire have shaped the earth into a work of unlikely splendor.

From a broad vista (opposite page) the work of nature looks to be rolling layers of earth and grass. But up close, water has eroded "cannonball concretions" into view at the north unit of Theodore Roosevelt National Park. And near Amidon, the forces of fire from burning coal veins caused huge rocks to heave and tumble into new, unruly resting places.

Upon close examination, petrified wood shows the rich grain of wood first inundated by primordial swamps and now preserved in the dry air of the badlands. Bill and JoAnn Lowman (below), who ranch north of Sentinel Butte, demonstrate the size of some remaining petrified logs.

The Little Missouri River's masterwork is the north unit of Theodore Roosevelt National Park. Ponderosa pines grow in the southern reaches of the badlands, here shown at the Hanson family's historic Logging Camp Ranch near Amidon. Horses remain the best — and often, the only — way to traverse the badlands terrain.

Bighorn sheep have been reintroduced in the badlands, where the original species that inspired the great naturalist Audubon was hunted to extinction. Their carefully monitored cousins now seem to be making a comeback. Among the most commonly seen long-term residents are bison, prairie dogs and mule deer. The abundant grasses and sheltered ravines of the south unit are so heavily populated with animals and birds that it often resembles a wildlife park.

29

Elk thrive in the south unit of Theodore Roosevelt National Park. During the mating season in autumn, visitors can glimpse males fighting for territory or to increase their harems. Experts believe the herd will grow large enough to spill out beyond the park into the badlands, eventually creating excellent big game hunting for western North Dakota.

Wild horses still roam the badlands, a living remnant of the days of the great ranches and open range. Equally successful are the wild turkeys that have been introduced to the area. Antelope seem to prefer the tenderer pastures of farmland, while the jackrabbit and coyote still play their age-old, deadly serious games of hide-and-seek.

Artist Karl Bodmer visited Fort Union, the premiere trading post of the fur trade era, as a member of the party accompanying Prince Maximilian upriver in 1833-34. The prince observed, "Fort Union was not just an outpost in the wilderness, but an elaborate group of wooden structures built as much to impress the Indian groups who came to trade as it was for defensive and security purposes." Today, an exact replica of the fort (including the bourgeois house, left) is under construction as an interpretive center documenting this first wave of capitalism in the American West.

Traders, Troops and Wagon Trains

The lonesome land of North Dakota's western margin was among the first corners of the American West to be explored . . . and one of the last to be settled.

In between the day the Lewis and Clark Expedition passed the junction of the Missouri and Yellowstone Rivers in 1805 and the hour of Sitting Bull's surrender at Fort Buford in 1881, the arid remote country remained the province of fur traders, Indians, the U.S. Army . . . and legends.

Throughout those critical years its reputation far outstripped its growth as a part of the still-new American nation. The Little Missouri Badlands entered the annals of the west less as the frontier of opportunity than as a wild foe.

Harsh and unpredictable, it was portrayed as a malevolent obstacle to the sort of civilizing, fortune-making dreams which fueled development of the golden west a thousand miles beyond. The harsh and rumpled land reared up before them like an untamed stallion. Unbroken to bit and saddle, it trumpeted a challenge that still rang out well into the twentieth century.

Throughout most of the 1800s the area hovered blank on schoolboys' maps, darkly identified as the Great American Desert. Along with its remote locale and inhospitable climate, it was perennially shadowed by tension between the Indians who claimed it and the armed encroachment of the U.S. government.

Who would want such country?

Men who longed for fortune.

Men who longed for adventure.

Men who longed to log answers across the mysterious heart of the North American continent.

Fur traders of the Hudson's Bay Company and its main competitors, the XY and North

West Companies, ventured southwest from their posts in British and French Canada in the last quarter of the eighteenth century. The Upper Missouri country served as a natural crossroads between Indians of present-day Montana's mountains and the Dakota plains. Hardships of the long mosquito-ridden journey from established posts in Canada were offset by the buffalo robes and beaver skins available there.

That brisk trade was upset when President Thomas Jefferson scrawled his name in an inky swash across the deed to the Louisiana Purchase. With that, the youthful United States double the land within its boundaries by acquiring France's entire New World holdings. As Napoleon put his stamp on the bargain, he's said to have snarled, "I have given to England a maritime rival that will sooner or later humble her pride."

At three cents per acre, the purchase of the Missouri River's drainage basin was the most dramatic real estate deal in American history. In practice, however, the humbling of British interests proceeded at a less hurried pace. Their eventual withdrawal had as much to do with the increasing burden of long-distance supply lines and stepped-up competition as it did with the unfurling of the seventeen-star American flag over badlands country.

The Corps of Volunteers for North-West Discovery — the Lewis and Clark Expedition — set off from St. Louis in mid-May of 1804. Charged with fulfilling Jefferson's dream by tracing the Missouri River to the western ocean, they and their men launched their keelboat and pirogues on an epic journey of exploration.'

They reached the junction of the Missouri and the Knife Rivers in late fall after fighting their way up 1,600 miles of turbulent muddy current on their 4,000-mile journey to the Pacific. There they settled in for the winter in a dozen cabins within a sturdy triangular stockade. They dubbed their camp Fort Man-

The annual Buckskinner Rendezvous at Fort Union attracts avid modern frontiersmen who with their families spend their days and nights just as fur trappers did in the days when the post was the gateway to the riches of the West.

dan in honor of their friendly neighbors, the Mandan Indians.

As winter waned the men continued up the increasingly narrow waterway. They reached the confluence of the Yellowstone and Missouri in the spring of 1805. Lewis noted in his journal that the beaver were larger, more abundant and "better clad" than any they had seen before. The faithful chronicler of natural marvels, he recorded observations on continual wind, petrified wood, alkali deposits along the bank, lignite coal and abundant buffalo. He added that the site on which they'd camped would be ideal for a trading post.

The promising news they carried back to the president in 1806 inspired St. Louis traders to add the Upper Missouri to their itineraries. Manuel Lisa, the earliest fur baron of the Upper Missouri, was among the first along with Andrew Henry, who ascended the river in 1808 as an emissary of the Missouri Fur Company, pushing beyond to the mountains.

Henry returned in 1822 with the Ashley-Henry Outfit, a collaboration with entrepreneur William Ashley. Fort Henry was built at the site that Merriwether Lewis had remarked upon, not far from where Williston stands today. But persistent problems with the Indians, both downriver and further west, forced a prudent halt to their venture. Their post was abandoned two years after it was built.

Most famous of all was Kenneth McKenzie, the shrewd Scotsman who founded Fort Floyd — soon renamed Fort Union — in 1828. He came to John Jacob Astor's American Fur Company by way of Canada, where he learned the fur trade with the Hudson's Bay and North West Companies. Their consolidation left him jobless, and so he looked to the United States.

Initially he opened trade along the Upper Missouri on behalf his own firm, the Columbia Fur Company, headquartered on Lake Traverse in Minnesota. Later merging with

Fort Union's traders preferred making their deals with their Indian customers outside its walls, where several tribes including the Assiniboines assembled after a successful hunting and trapping season. The Mandan chief Four Bears (right), "mighty in council and mightier in war," was revered by Indians and whites alike. He well understood the unique importance of the Indian trade to the white economy. Claimed by the smallpox epidemic of 1837, he is memorialized in the name of the bridge spanning Lake Sakakawea at New Town.

Astor's organization and gaining access to his unlimited capital, McKenzie pushed on to dominate Upper Missouri trade from his post a few miles from the mouth of the Yellowstone.

McKenzie was a tough and ingenious businessman, ruling an extent of country greater than many notable empires in history. He lived an untamed variation of the aristocratic life in his distant outpost, dressing for the dinners served each evening on fine china, crystal and silver. Butter, chocolate, fine French brandy and cigars were regular fare at his table. He reigned over his prosperous company with bizarre dash and a keen eye to his profits.

Trade with the Indians was a cutthroat and often unscrupulous business. Despite proscription by the U.S. Congress, alcohol was a standard currency of exchange. It was used to buy customers' good will both by McKenzie (and other American traders) and personnel of the British Hudson's Bay Company, with whom he still competed for the Indian trade. Even the traders, heavy-drinking men well accustomed to violence, were awed by its effect on their native American clientele.

If the demoralizing influence of liquor took a heavy toll on the Indian people who bought it with their buffalo robes and beaver pelts, still it was only a taste of the desolation to come.

First sight of the sidewheel steamer Yellowstone in 1832 belching fire and steam had convinced many of the prairie people of the white man's unearthly power. Only five years later they felt the invisible impact of a far more awesome force that he unleashed among them.

Smallpox arrived upriver in 1837 on the deck of the steamer St. Peter. It infected native and newcomer alike with the hellish scourge. But while many of the white traders and trappers had some natural resistance to the disease, the Indians had none. Whites often recovered. Indian people did not.

Uncounted tens of thousands died across the high plains. The villages of the Mandan and Hidatsa were hit hardest, the nomadic Sioux somewhat less. Between the first and subsequent epidemics, the region's population was drastically reduced. The succession of fathomless personal tragedies, layer upon layer of them, added up to more than sorrows. They led to a shift in the balance of power between the once rich and powerful Indian and the first wave of Americans doing business beneath the stars and stripes.

Trappers, traders, frontiersmen and adventurers of the mid-1800s traveled the Missouri to its confluence with the Yellowstone near present-day Williston, where the National Park Service is restoring the historically vital site of Fort Union. The original post was dismantled in 1867, well after the age of the fur trade had waned; its timbers were used to build nearby Fort Buford.

The rough badlands terrain stymied General Alfred Sully's 1864 Army campaign against the Sioux whom he found encamped west of the Missouri. As the Indians melted into the shadows, the soldiers instead destroyed their winter supplies of buffalo meat, their tipis and equipment. Several groups of military buffs (left) each year take part in "living history" reenactments, reliving the days of cavalry charges and infantry drills.

Western North Dakota first felt the American military presence in 1825, when General Henry Atkinson led a flotilla of some 500 soldiers upriver in keelboats from Iowa to the Knife River village. Another, smaller military expedition led by Major Isaac Stevens in 1853 visited Fort Union while surveying the northernmost of five routes proposed for railway links with the Pacific coast.

Within the bounds of today's North Dakota, white traders and their Indian clientele managed to maintain the uneasy status quo until the 1860s. Then the discovery of gold along the Fraser River in British Columbia, in Idaho and among the mountains of Montana magnified the traffic across the plains.

Fortune-seekers booked passage on steamboats and wagon trains bound for the gold fields of Virginia City, Bannack, Helena and beyond. James Fisk stopped at Fort Union with the first convoy of Minnesota wagons bound across Dakota Territory in 1862. During the next five years, seven other expeditions followed, some traversing the badlands and others choosing a variety of alternate routes in an attempt to avoid clashes with the increasingly militant Sioux.

The U.S. Army was committed to protecting these perhaps — foolhardy gold seekers as they nervously rolled across the prairie, circling their wagons each evening against its vast solitude. It took the Minnesota Sioux uprising of 1862, though, to bring the simmering pot to a full boil.

In 1863 Generals Alfred Sully and Henry Sibley swept across eastern Dakota with combined forces of some 5,000 men to punish the Indians. Between them, they engaged in half a dozen battles from the James River to the Missouri. (Subsequently, historians have noted that few if any of the hundreds of Sioux men, women and children who died had anything to do with the killing of whites along the Minnesota River that had inspired the Army campaigns.)

The U.S. troops returned in 1864 with Sully at the lead. Their objectives were threefold — to further punish the Sioux, to drive them from the routes taken by wagon trains, and to establish a line of forts for their future protection.

Sully's force came up the Missouri by steamboat, establishing North Dakota's first military post, Fort Rice, above the mouth of the Cannonball River. They proceeded overland toward the northwest, trailed by a wagon train led by Thomas Holmes which they'd encountered crossing the river.

Near Richardton the soldiers ordered the civilians to wait at the rear while they advanced toward Killdeer Mountain. There they found the Sioux bands they'd been hunting. Artillery buffeted the encampments until the Indians disappeared into the shadowy recesses of the badlands. The soldiers destroyed hundreds of tipis and other equip-

ment and burned an estimated 200 tons of buffalo meat the Indians had preserved for winter stores.

The troops trailed the Sioux well into the badlands, laboring over and around the weird terrain. A second battle was fought near Medora. The Indians, on the familiar ground they'd long favored for wintering, again melted into the brushy ravines along the Little Missouri.

Then Sully — facing a landscape even more formidable than his quarry — called off the pursuit. Instead he and his men destroyed the Indians' remaining supplies and rode on to Fort Union. Their return route carried them past Fort Berthold — a trading post built at the Three Tribes' request in 1845 — and downriver toward home.

Fort Rice hosted a second emigrant wagon train that summer, led by the veteran Captain James Fisk. Fisk was frustrated to learn that Sully's force had headed west with his rival Holmes' expedition in tow. Despite the Army's insistence that he follow a safer path, Fisk and his wagons set out along a southwesterly route, more direct than the usual arc up toward Fort Union.

All was peaceful for one hundred miles.

Only monuments remain on this lonely sweep of prairie to commemorate those who died during the two-week siege of a wagon train of gold-seekers headed toward Montana. Known as Fort Dilts, the site offers mute testimony of the perseverance of early civilian travelers facing hostile Sioux bands, impossibly rough terrain and scant protection from the elements.

Then, near the present site of Rhame, a band of Sioux warriors attacked the last two of the train's eighty wagons, killing a dozen men.

Fisk led his party on for two perilous days under continuous attack. Finally they dug in to defend themselves behind a six-foot rampart of sod they christened Fort Dilts (after scout Jefferson Dilts, a casualty of the battle). A small delegation left in the dead of night to summon Sully's help. Two miserable weeks later — well after their tormentors had lost interest and left the vicinity — the cavalry arrived to escort the hapless travelers back to Fort Rice.

Three more forts arose along the Missouri: Fort Buford in 1866 (built with timbers from Fort Union, abandoned with the end of the fur trade), Fort Stevenson near Fort Berthold in 1867, and Fort McKeen (later Fort Lincoln) in

1872. Each would play a part in the climax of the war between the U.S. Army and the Plains Indians.

Fort Stevenson would protect the decimated ranks of the Mandan, Hidatsa and Arikara nations from the great enemy they shared in common — the Sioux, the well-armed warriors rushing on horseback toward the critical events in high plains history.

George Armstrong Custer and the Seventh Cavalry would set out from Fort Lincoln for the Black Hills in 1874, discovering gold in mountains sacred to the Sioux and setting a course for desolation. Two years later, they'd head west through the badlands toward the Little Bighorn River to meet the greatest fighting force the Indians ever mustered.

And Fort Buford would mark the beginning and the end of the war for the plains.

Sitting Bull and his band of warriors admonished troops of the Sixth Infantry to leave in haste even as they laid the fort's foundations. Many of the same military personnel — whom the legendary Indian leader had first dismissed as little more than a nuisance — would be on hand, fourteen years later, to see a proud foe yield to the forces of history.

Scourged unceasingly by the Army in the wake of Custer's epic defeat, Sitting Bull and a small band of followers retreated to Canada in 1877. Four years later the tired, hungry band reappeared at the gates of Fort Buford. Handing over his gun, he told the assembled witnesses, *"I wish it to be remembered that I was the last man of my tribe to surrender my rifle."*

Sitting Bull's band of Sioux (above) surrendered at Fort Buford on July 20, 1881 . . . a historic event considered the last chapter in the war between the Plains Indians and the U.S. Army. The ragged, hungry band was the last to yield to reservation life. Eight years later Sitting Bull — then a resident of the Standing Rock Reservation — would march in North Dakota's statehood parade and tour with Buffalo Bill Cody's Wild West Show, signing autographs for a dollar apiece.

Reservation life (top left) was harsh for tribes accustomed to the freedom of the plains. This 1897 photo records the issue of rations to Indians on the Fort Berthold Reservation. The role of Fort Buford, once a significant site in the settling of the West (lower left), diminished as hostilities ceased.

With Lt. Col. George Armstrong Custer at the head, the Seventh Cavalry column moved out from Fort Abraham Lincoln in 1876 on its fateful journey to the Little Big Horn. The cavalry marched through the badlands, camping just south of present-day Medora and passing through the modern site of Beach. Efforts to rebuild the fort received a boost when the commander's nephew Charles Armstrong Custer (above) lent his support to the project.

CUSTER HOME

This was the site of the dwelling occupied by Gen. George A. Custer Commanding Officer of Fort Abraham Lincoln from 1873 until his death at the battle of the Little Big Horn on June 25-1876

The legend of Standing Rock is told on a monument overlooking Lake Oahe at Fort Yates (above). It is said to resemble a Sioux woman and her child who refused to accompany their tribe on a journey; when the rest returned to find them, all that remained was this rock. The great Sioux medicine man Sitting Bull (upper right) gave spiritual guidance to the Plains tribes who awaited Custer in the Little Big Horn Valley. His grave at Fort Yates (lower right) has been repeatedly vandalized; there's some doubt about where his bones rest today.

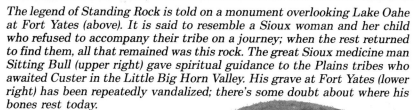

43

Mindful of their heritage, badlands ranchers today work a roundup much like their grandfathers did, on horseback, trailing cattle through the rough terrain. When the cattle reach the ranch, neighbors turn out to help rope, brand and vaccinate the calves. As much an occasion to work as to socialize, branding days usually rotate from ranch to ranch in late May and early June until everyone has finished working their cattle.

The Last Virgin Range

"*A*ll *through this region there has been a scanty and sparse settlement, quite peculiar in its character,*" Theodore Roosevelt wrote in <u>Century</u> Magazine in 1888.

"*In the forest the woodchopper comes first; on the fertile prairie the granger is the pioneer; but on the long stretching uplands of the far West is the men who guard and follow the horned herds that prepare the way for the settlers who come after.*"

Fewer than a thousand badlands cowboys who guarded half a million cattle caught the imagination of settled America, thrilling staid armchair adventurers who read of their exploits in the claustrophobic comfort of gaslit Victorian parlors. For one brief decade of glory spent a century ago, western Dakota's ranching country moved to center stage in the chronicles of the American West.

Here was drama of the highest order: Magnificent dreams tempered by the grit of reality. Here, too, were characters drawn larger than life, nearly on par to challenge the mountain man legend of Mike Fink or the apocryphal Paul Bunyan.

There were the Marquis de Mores, the French millionaire aristocrat who sank his fortune into an impossible dream, and Theodore Roosevelt, the wheezing young easterner whom the badlands made a man. There were wealthy eastern sportsmen who returned to found great ranches, along with buckskinned notables like the Billings County sheriff, Hell-Roarin' Bill Jones, and crack rifleman Gerry Paddock, a gambler and hunter who knew the far side of the law.

They flourished in the wild Dakota of roundups and shoot'em-ups, of rustlers and prairie

The Northern Pacific Railroad pushed west across the Missouri in 1879. That year a detachment of soldiers was assigned to the badlands to protect the N.P. crews. They threw up tents and rude log cabins on the west bank of the Little Missouri and called it Cantonment Bad Lands.

Railway construction passed the fledgling camp of Dickinson and pushed on to Little Missouri, as the soldiers' site was known, in the fall of 1880. The post trader, genial Frank Moore, opened up the Pyramid Park Hotel just as the river began to freeze, welcoming the first of the hunting parties drawn west by N.P. advertisements.

The brushy draws and ravines were one of the last spots in the Great Plains still thickly populated by big game, not only buffalo but elk, deer, antelope and even bears. Among the intrepid easterners who first took up the challenge were two Pennsylvanians, Howard Eaton and A.C. Huidekoper, and a New York City tenderfoot named Roosevelt.

The trophies which gave them cause to boast were modest compared to the game bagged by professional hunters. In just two seasons, the pros had reduced the bison herds to scattered remnants, scattering the prairies with ripening carcasses and bones.

Even as they stalked their prey, the most perceptive marksmen were coming to realize an even greater resource lay in the dry brown prairie grass beneath their feet. Unlike the rich moist pastures of the East and Middle West, this prairie hay cured on the stem, banking its nutritional value for winter grazing on the sheltered badlands ranges. The locomotives that carried carloads of hunters on safari could transport cattle and capitalists willing to put up funds to exploit the untouched land.

Sportsmen returned to establish ranches,

The Northern Pacific Railroad campaigned to lure hunters to what promoters called Pyramid Park, building a hotel at the site of Bad Land City. Ranch hands pose in front of the bunkhouse at the HT Ranch, one of the earliest to capitalize on the virgin range along the Little Missouri River (right).

rattlers, of hunters who bagged grizzlies and a thousand head of buffalo per season in the raw rugged land of the last virgin prairie.

For a time, ranch life in the badlands country resembled the romantic notions of western fiction — a parallel so true that famed cowboy movie star Tom Mix married his sweetheart at the foot of the dun-colored bluff that keeps Medora in violet shadow long after the dawn.

It was a rugged way of life . . . and yet too fragile to survive. As young Roosevelt observed, ranchers opened up the Little Missouri country to the settlers who followed, bringing with them deeds and fences and families and the end to the saga of the open range.

An early hunter displays pelts of wolf, coyote, lynx and bobcat in front of his badlands cabin, testimony to the accuracy of railroad boasts about good hunting. Foreman Robert Hanson (right) shows off his prize mount at the Logging Camp Ranch near Amidon, established by cattle baron H.C. Huidekoper for raising horses and later purchased by Hanson. Tools of the trade are close at hand: lariat, quirt, tall leather boots, neckerchief and broad-brimmed hat.

Cowboys worked the Marquis de Mores' livestock near Medora. During roundup, all available hands coordinated their efforts under an appointed boss who supervised branding of stock found in territory claimed by each rancher. Riders often worked the area from Grassy Butte to Fort Yates, branding several thousand head on the open range in a single season.

and hunters remained to work them. Among the first was A.C. Huidekoper, who ran cattle on his HT spread south of Medora and raised horses at the Logging Camp Ranch near Amidon, and the Eaton Brothers, whose Custer Trail Ranch catered to later greenhorns as the nation's first dude ranch.

Seized by the beauty and challenge of badlands life, Roosevelt returned to plunge into the cattle business with characteristic vigor. He invested in the Maltese Cross Ranch south of Medora in 1883 with local partners Sylvane Ferris and A.W. Merrifield handling the operation. A year later he added the Elkhorn Ranch thirty-five miles north of the cowtown, bringing Bill Sewall and Wilmot Dow out from Maine to manage it.

The dashing Marquis de Mores arrived in Medora, too, in 1883, with dreams of multiplying his fortune. Backed by ten million dollars in capital, he set out not only to raise cows between the buttes, but to slaughter them in

Medora and ship prime beef east in refrigerated cars for the ever-growing consumer market.

Word traveled south as well as east. The big Texas cattle companies set their sights on the ungrazed Little Missouri prairie. Hundreds of thousands of steers bearing the famous brands of the OX, Three Sevens, Long X and Hash Knife were herded a thousand miles north along the branching Chisholm Trail. The largest outfit, the Hash Knife, alone ran sixty thousand head. Still more cattle rolled in from Minnesota and Iowa on the N.P. line, until an estimated half a million were grazing on the grasslands south and west of the Missouri.

Like all the rest, the future president fattened his stock on land in the public domain or owned by the railroad. None of the ranchers held deeds to the vast property they controlled. Instead, the unwritten code of the west gave them use of their "customary range" by

publishing the boundaries of the acreage they'd chosen in a newspaper along with their brand.

Within two or three years the grasslands were pushed far beyond their capacity to support the ravenous cattle. Unlike the fifty million bison that once roamed the length and breadth of the Great Plains, these beeves munched and trampled the same meadows four seasons of the year. Nor were they cut out for the severe winters for which the buffalo had been well-suited.

For several years they chomped and multiplied unthreatened, thanks to unusually mild winters and abundant forage. But the contrary climate reasserted itself in the winter of 1886-1887. Snow drifted five feet deep in the Little Missouri bottoms; blizzards buffeted the luckless cows, and the chilled and weakened animals quickly froze or slowly starved by the hundreds of thousands.

When the snow finally receded, the plains

were ripe with the choking odor of death. The gentleman ranchers were sobered by the hideous sight. After surveying his losses Roosevelt wrote a friend, *"For the first time, I have been utterly unable to enjoy a visit to my ranch. I shall be glad to get home."* Though he continued to visit the badlands occasionally, he never recaptured the electrifying sense of optimism and adventure that had marked his glorious years as a cowboy.

The Texas outfits pulled back after losing three-quarters of their cattle. They and others who remained reduced the scale of their herds and introduced better management practices, including rotating their herds from upland in summer to the winter shelter of buttes and stockpiling hay for emergencies.

No hard-won lessons in animal husbandry, however, could dim the writing on the bunkhouse wall: Though many lingered until the turn of the century, the day of the great open-range ranches was over. In the next years they would be supplanted by far smaller operations carved out by immigrant families hoping to find a better life on the same arid grasslands that exacted so high a price.

The rough-riding cowboys would grow older and settle down. They'd revel in epic accounts of freedom and glory told to the next generation of young men, forever engrossed in the rip-snorting saga that ended in the icy snow.

During the days that followed Roosevelt's heartsick parting with the Little Missouri country he loved, he too continued telling the cowboys' tales — some tall, some true — for an eager eastern audience of readers entranced with the West.

He concluded his popular series in <u>Century</u> Magazine with a tribute to the hardy men he so admired: *"To appreciate properly his fine, manly qualities, the wild rough-rider of the plains should be seen in his own home. There he passes his days; there he does his life-work;* *there, when he meets death, he faces it as he has faced many other evils, with quiet uncomplaining fortitude.*

"Brave, hospitable, hardy, and adventurous, he is the grim pioneer of our race; he prepares the way for the civilization from before whose face he must himself disappear. Hard and dangerous though his existence is, it has yet a wild attraction that strongly draws to it his bold, free spirit.

"He lives in the lonely lands where mighty rivers twist in long reaches between the barren bluffs; where the prairies stretch out into billowy plains of waving grass, girt only by the blue horizon — plains across whose endless breadth he can steer his course for days and weeks and see neither man to speak to nor hill to break the level; where the glory and the burning splendor of the sunsets kindle the blue vault of heaven and the level brown earth till they merge together in an ocean of flaming fire."

Ranch women — (from left) Maude Collis, Edith Collis Hanson and Hattie Collis holding baby James — worked as hard as men. They planted the gardens, raised the children, tended the animals, educated the young, and brought a touch of civilization home to the rough country. An infrequent trip to town (left) sometimes meant shopping for supplies enough to last through the winter. . .or most of next year. Fresh horses were broken before roundup (above), with cowboys training mounts for their own remudas. But challenging wild steeds, as in this rodeo photo from the Amidon area, was also a way to whittle away hours awaiting the real work to begin.

Hunters and cattle barons were the first in the badlands, but sheepherders like this rancher from the Amidon-Hettinger area were also numerous. Shepherds lived a lonely life, trailing their herds with small wagons equipped with bedding, a cook stove and supplies to last for months.

He was darkly handsome, daring, ambitious . . . and in love with the woman whose name he gave to the unofficial capital of the Little Missouri Badlands.

She was a lovely New York heiress, young enough to share his impetuous visions.

Together the Marquis and Marquise de Mores forged the badlands' classic story of romance. Today the richly appointed chateau they built high above the sluggish river looks down on their curious legacy: A tiny cow town that still carries her name, and a towering brick chimney alone in a rumpled meadow, all that remains of her husband's dream to make a fortune in the wilderness.

Antoine de Vallombrosa, the French aristocrat, had great plans for the badlands. Here he would not only raise prime beef but slaughter it, ship it in refrigerated cars to the East Coast, and — by sidestepping middlemen along the way — capture the lion's share of the market with his lower prices.

He founded a new town across the river from Little Missouri and christened it Medora in honor of his wife, smashing a bottle of fine French champagne over an iron tent peg. Local wags, not altogether impressed with the dynamic but headstrong newcomer, noted with delight that the ceremony occurred on April Fool's Day.

The village bustled almost instantly, fed by a stream of workers recruited to build the first of de Mores' slaughtering plants and tend cattle and sheep on his forty-five thousand acres of prime river bottomland.

But his local enterprise was only one small element of a far greater scheme. Backed by ten million dollars raised among New York financiers, he went on to construct two more slaughtering plants in Billings and Miles City and buy others in Seattle, Portland, Winnipeg and Kansas City. He built or bought cold-storage warehouses in Bismarck, Fargo, Duluth, Helena, Miles City, Glendive, Brainerd and Minneapolis; founded the Northern Pacific Refrigerator Car Company, and, with Andrew and R.B. Mellon, formed a bank in Bismarck.

Nor did he limit his enterprises to the beef industry. He founded Medora's newspaper, the Bad Lands Cow Boy, and established a stage line between Medora and the gold fields of the Black Hills. In the town itself he built a church, a school, a theatre, and clubrooms for his employes and their families equipped a bowling alley. Beyond all this, he bought twenty thousand acres of wheat land near Bismarck and offered it tax-free to settlers who would farm it and build up the country.

With Medora and their children, he lived the hybrid life of an aristocrat and an industrialist, oddly transposed on the windswept brown-and-grey prairie. They entertained in stately grace but also hunted bear together; she painted delicate watercolors but loved galloping even more across the upland prairie.

But even as all seemed prosperous and serene, trouble approached from several quarters. Locally, resentment against the uppity foreigner de Mores built to a fever pitch. It culminated in charges of murder brought against him for the shooting of a rustler. Though he was eventually acquitted after a spectacular trial in Bismarck, it was clear that he was not welcome, at least in parts of the badlands neighborhood.

More seriously still, his beef-packing enterprise was beset by problems. Competitors, fearing the loss of their own markets, undercut the prices of his beef. At the same time, rumors spread among consumers that the refrigerated meat was somehow poisoned; even those who knew better found his range-fed beef less palatable than richer meat from cattle finished on grains.

In less than three years it was all over. The chateau, furnishings and all, looked over the valley with shuttered eyes. De Mores kept his packing plant at Medora open long enough to repay his investors, then closed its doors, absorbing a personal loss of several million dollars.

For years a sign hung upon its door saying "Rent free to any responsible party who will make use of it."

No one ever did.

The Chateau de Mores

All that remains of de Mores' grand dreams for the town of Medora is a sculpted likeness in the town square and his chateau, lavishly furnished by western standards with imported wines, a piano, elegant furniture and trunk after trunk packed with clothing. The dining room was the scene for many convivial dinners with his contemporaries including fellow rancher Theodore Roosevelt. Servants stood by awaiting the diners' every need at meals that often lasted four hours.

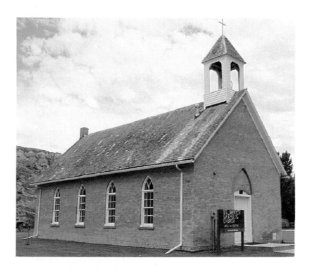

Fire destroyed de Mores' packing plant in Medora, the final blow to an already-doomed venture. In many ways the Marquis' scheme made sense, but the marketplace ultimately rejected his vision. Others of his gifts to the city remain, including the church where his wife worshipped — still used for services today — and the fine house to accommodate visits by his in-laws, the wealthy Von Hoffmans of New York, today a museum housing an extensive collection of dolls.

Theodore Roosevelt stepped off a Northern Pacific train in Little Missouri at 2 a.m. on the day after the "Golden Spike Special" had barreled through, headed for the ceremony in Montana marking the line's completion.

His goal, he said, was to hunt buffalo "while there are still buffalo to hunt." Twenty-four years old, asthmatic and voraciously curious about all things natural in the outdoors, he took to the badlands with glee: Here was a land where the air was as effervescent and dry as champagne, where adventures could be launched far larger than life, and where he could live the rugged manly life far from his patrician past and the political maneuverings that presaged his future.

His delight in the badlands bridged the social gulf between himself and the men he met there. As for Roosevelt, he could not get enough of the country. On that first trip he invested perhaps half of his modest wealth in the Maltese Cross Ranch near Chimney Butte.

He returned to New York to serve his third term in its legislature and to become embroiled in Republican national politics. But the year turned hideously dark. His mother Mittie died in the small hours of the morning; by mid-afternoon, his wife Alice had also passed away. The date: Valentine's Day, 1884.

Still sorrowing for them and stinging from the defeat of his reform candidate for the presidential nomination, he headed west to forget his troubles. He wrote of those days, *"Nowhere, not even at sea, does a man feel more lonely than when riding over the far-reaching, seemingly never-ending plains. Their vastness and loneliness and their melancholy monotony have a strong fascination . . . ."*

He headed north alone on his horse Manitou looking for complete solitude in which he could write, read poetry, tend his cattle and recover his spirits. He found it thirty-five miles north of Medora at what became his Elkhorn Ranch.

Over the next two years he alternated between the simple, invigorating routine he carved out of the badlands and the dense political tangles back in New York. When the life of a gentleman became too complex, he'd retreat to Dakota Territory to take part in round-ups, hunt to his heart's content, and defend the rough-and-ready code of frontier justice. Along the way he earned the respect of his rugged colleagues, a victory he valued even above his success on the national scene.

Eyes flashing behind his spectacles, he was inevitably known as Old Four-Eyes. But for a tenderfoot who convulsed the cowboys early on with his urgent command to "hasten quickly there, my good man," he won a satisfying measure of acceptance. It inspired and moved him for the rest of his life.

Addressing a political rally in Fargo in 1910, he noted that he'd passed through 27 years before on his first trip to the badlands, where he spent the happiest and most profitable years of his life. *"If it had not been for what I learned during those years here in North Dakota, I would never in the world have been president of the United States,"* he said, and added, *"I'm thrilled to be home again."*

Theodore Roosevelt arrived in Medora the typical eastern dude, but left a seasoned cattleman and enthusiastic fan of the West . . . summed up by his comment to a hunting guide, "By Godfrey, isn't this fun!"

Roosevelt's first badlands home was the Maltese Cross Ranch, whose ranchhouse now stands on the grounds of the National Park Service's visitors center. The cabin was typical of those of the 1880s, with sparse furnishings intended to be practical, functional and durable. Along with his riding, hunting and cowpunching, Roosevelt spent his days reading poetry and writing about the ways of the West.

Medora boomed in the 1880s, thanks to the free-spending Marquis de Mores who poured millions of dollars into its economy. His packing plant dominated the landscape and was the town's principal employer. He also founded the Medora-Deadwood stage line; one of its coaches is preserved in the interpretive center near his chateau. Remnants of Tepee Bottom Ranch (right) are reminders of one of the first spreads in badlands country.

For 80 years the Osborns of Dickinson chronicled daily lives and historic occasions in western North Dakota. Their legacy today offers a rare glimpse into another time.

A.J. "Josh" Osborn established his photography studio in 1896. He displayed a keen eye for people and events, along with a knack for crisp images of the badlands — often sold as murals for the region's banks. His son Lawton carried on the business, followed in turn by a grandson, Lawton "Buzz" Osborn Jr., who finally sold the business in 1976.

Along with portraits and wedding photographs, the three enjoyed recording everyday scenes on badlands ranches. Many of their works are currently being compiled for exhibition by Larry Brown of Fargo.

Lawton Osborn stopped at Gus Bell's barn near Medora in the spring of 1934, knowing that little ranch work was done at that time of year and that a "blind pig" was rumored to be on the premises. He found a card game in process. Though some props were added for effect (note the handgun on the table), the photo recorded the scene virtually as Osborn found it. Pictured from left to right are Dutch Ziegler, an unidentified boy and rancher, Gus's son Eddie, and Medora rancher Billy Neuens.

Two photographs taken only a few years apart but representing two very different cultures demonstrate the Osborns' keen eye for details. The Gros Ventre woman at left displayed her fine beadwork and ceremonial garb for a studio portrait in 1917. "Lady at Ease," at right, was used to advertise a Dickinson historic pageant about 1908.

True to their reputation, the Osborns attended countless roundups and brandings. Cowboys and visiting bankers or businessmen pose together before the chuckwagon on Wallis Huidekoper's roundup on Ash Coulee ten miles south of Dickinson.

Even in the 1950's, a badlands wild horse roundup (top) spelled excitement. The New York Times published this Osborn photo. Other assignments were less dramatic, but the Osborns carried on, as in a pair of photos of badlands cowboys in Dickinson for a good time. After a bath, haircut and shave, the hands usually had a photo taken to send back home to Mother or give to a local sweetheart. The photos include "The Dude" (far left), circa 1900; and "Drinking Buddies," circa 1909.

(Overleaf) Cowboys move cattle into a corral at the Logging Camp Ranch.

Texas longhorn cattle were first to graze on the grasses of the Little Missouri River. The Long X Bridge near Grassy Butte was built to enable large herds to cross the sluggish river. Today a few longhorns are still raised in the badlands, but the open range country is commonly home for more modern breeds like Herefords (below) and Angus.

Spring's crop of newborn calves is vital to the badlands rancher, who must check his herd daily. Bill Lowman of Sentinel Butte hunts for his spurs while his wife JoAnn plays with a new litter of kittens. He must tag and number each calf, often over the verbal objections of its mother, and see that ample water and feed is at hand in his pastures.

Roundups take place in late spring, with neighbors gathering on weekends to help work each other's cattle. Cows and calves are gathered, driven to pens on the ranch, sorted, branded and vaccinated.

Many hands make reasonably light work, even of branding several hundred anxious calves. First the calves are roped, dragged into a pen and wrestled to the ground by two or three cowboys. They're then branded, dehorned and — if the calf in question is a bull — changed by means of a cutter into a steer. The hot iron leaves each rancher's distinctive brand on his calves' hide, but causes no pain to the animal.

Although there's plenty of work to be done, roundups are also social. Neighbors gather to visit, tell tales and joke about who's working hardest or doing the worst job of roping . . . all in good fun. Ed Willson and Harold Lowman (top right), two old-timers of the Sentinel Butte area, share some observations on the weather. Jim Tescher of Medora (below right), a former professional rodeo champion, talks with Lusk Lowman. Neighbors Tyler Cook and Rod Brown (above) take a break to observe another's roping problems. Wives are busy behind the scenes laying out a generous spread of food and cold drinks for an afternoon picnic.

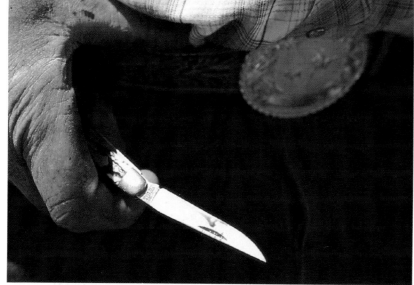

The Logging Camp Ranch, long in the Hanson family, got its name from an early attempt to cut native Ponderosa pine and float them downsteam to Medora. Today the former horse ranch is highly diversified, raising cattle and crops, harvesting pine for log home construction, and welcoming guests to a few rustic tourist cabins.

Under the gaze of hundreds of visiting automotive and travel writers, the Hansons demonstrate how the Dodge Dakota pickup comes in handy in ranching. The guests were part of a promotion surrounding the new model's 1987 introduction.

71

The Snowden Bridge spans the Missouri near Williston. Until 1985 it was shared daily by Burlington Northern trains and automobile drivers going about their business at the confluence of the Missouri and Yellowstone. The Fairview bridge (opposite) crosses the Yellowstone, allowing river navigation below with a 300-foot lift span. These two are the only lift-span bridges in North Dakota. Another "only" is logged by the 1,456-foot Fairview railroad tunnel, the sole one in the state.

Opening the West

Western Dakota's first residents were not the kind to settle down and raise up cities.

From roaming bands of Plains Indians to the first white men they met there, it was a land whose culture denied the need for permanent roots. French, British, Spanish and American traders established posts at strategic points in the wilderness intent on building fortunes, not towns. Soldiers surged across the Missouri River with short-term campaigns in mind. They anticipated nothing so eagerly as their departure.

North Dakota's major eastern and central cities were well-established and rural settlement already in progress when the first permanent communities began to lay foundations in the west. As they did all through the northern half of Dakota Territory, they sprang up along with the railroads, sometimes spontaneously but more often as part of their business plans.

The Northern Pacific mainline reached the Montana border in late 1880, pushing on toward completion in 1883. James J. Hill's Great Northern Railroad arrived at Williston and moved beyond in 1887. But neither occasion was marked by a flurry of civic activity — nor would they be for decades.

The first to arrive throughout the west were ranchers. Many of them grazed cattle on a scale to rival the bonanza farms of the Red River Valley. Like those gargantuan wheat farms, they were owned by outside investors and fueled by enormous capital. But the ranchers had one big advantage: they took up public lands, avoiding even the pocket-change price that easterners paid for their acreage.

By their very nature, the big-time ranchers were impermanent in western Dakota, as they were throughout the plains. When

Settlement followed the railroads into North Dakota's western margin. The arid land and tortuous badlands made the region especially dependent upon the railroads, crossing rivers and opening new territory for homesteaders. Railroad construction in McKenzie County (above) opened an area aptly named for famed N.P. Railroad lobbyist and political boss Alexander McKenzie; the railroad ferry (below) served the same county. An immigrant train (above) unloads its cargo of settlers and possessions in Hettinger in 1908.

smaller ranching and farming families came to make the land their home, the big outfits first resisted and then moved on.

The large ranchers' interests were best served by locating as far from their neighbors as they could get. It was not a pattern of land use geared to building a sense of community or founding civic services. They didn't want them; they didn't need them; and, in fact, they fought smaller ranchers and farmers for years to prevent organization of local units of government which would tax their cattle to build the roads, bridges and schools they considered irrelevent to their way of life.

Until the turn of the century they had the region mostly to themselves. Despite railroad promotion and the arrival of several major land companies, the west-river country had failed to draw many pioneers. The few towns that had sprung up mirrored the ranchers' needs, providing access to transportation and a source for kitchen staples, ranch supplies, ammunition and hell-raising Saturday nights.

Dickinson, where a post office was established in 1881, was a major Northern Pacific shipping point from the beginning, along with rival Sully Springs eight miles east of Medora. Its first inbound cargo was gentlemen hunters and Minnesota cattle to fatten on the range; outbound, it carried tons of buffalo robes, beef and later buffalo bones.

Williston, first known as Little Muddy, was inspired by the Great Northern's arrival in 1887. It was a rough tent colony with a saloon on every corner of its single business block and seven others scattered in between. The town was not incorporated until 1894.

The real town-raising began with the arrival of steady stream of pioneer families and merchants, first clinging to the railroads' course and, only when those lands were taken, beginning to tackle the dry, broken prairie. Some groups of land-seekers from the eastern U.S. and Russia did begin filing into the area before North Dakota's statehood —

Fervid bidding marked an auction of town lots in Bowman in 1907. After the railroad opened a region, it did its best to help settlement along by establishing a townsite every few miles. While the locomotives took on coal and water, trainmen unloaded mail, settlers and supplies. Every town had its incurable optimists who used the local weekly newspaper to trumpet predictions that their city would soon be the next great metropolis between Minneapolis and the West Coast ... extravagant claims that turned out to be patently untrue.

among them, evangelical Germans to Hebron, Catholic German-Russians to Richardton, families from the northeastern states to New England (originally named Mayflower), and members of a Christian sect from Ripon, Wis., to Gladstone. For most of the area, however, the arrivals picked up steam after 1900.

The western lands themselves were one of the causes for the delay. While the tracks and some of the future townsites were in place for at least part of the great Dakota boom of the 1880s, few land-seeking farmers pushed beyond the Missouri River.

To the east, soils were richer, rains fell more predictably, and civilization seemed to lie closer to the eastern horizon. The west came with no such reassurances. Early surveyors had estimated that no more than half the land was suitable for agriculture, the rest more apt for grazing livestock. The lawless aura of Indian warfare and frontier justice clung to the region; and — most significantly — the railroads were still engaged in selling their lands and promoting their townsites in the Red River Valley and the rolling central terrain.

Inevitably the demand for land built up and washed across the Missouri Slope. The big

ranchers who remained after the disastrous winter of 1886-87 began to feel the pressure from smaller operators. Some started to acquire title to their land and even put up fences to defend their holdings. But buying land meant not only investing capital but paying taxes on it.

Nor was government to be held back much longer. Small ranchers and farmers led a movement to organize McKenzie County in the early 1900s. Angry resistance from large ranchers held it off for a few years, but in 1905 the state legislature stepped in and settled the matter. (They commemorated the rowdy tenor of the time by naming it for political boss Alex McKenzie; its first town was christened Alexander.)

The western margin of North Dakota settled down to serious building on the eve of the twentieth century.

Railroad construction gangs were on the move again. Branch lines began to snake out north and south from the Great Northern and Northern Pacific mainlines. The Milwaukee, St. Paul and Sault St. Marie — the Soo Line — extended diagonally toward the northwest. The Chicago, Milwaukee and St. Paul sent tendrils into the southwestern corner.

Wherever the railroads stretched, they carried the contagion for town-booming. The rather late date of their arrival affected what settlement did exist along their paths. East of the river, they often arrived first and charted towns. West of the river and north to Canada, they extended into a region already thinly populated with struggling settlements. Nevertheless, location along a railroad line remained a principle goal of their fledgling city fathers.

If the railroads would not come to a townsite . . . well, the townsite might well go to the railroad. That was the story along each of the

lines. Perhaps the most dramatic example was at Crosby.

Founded in 1903, the village had begun to flourish when, three years later, the Soo Line came through one mile to the east. Crosby residents watched in envy as railroad officials created a competing town they called Imperial. Some settlers had already relocated there when the Great Northern, too, pushed deeper into Divide County — passing one mile west of Old Crosby.

North Dakota towns dreamed of having a railroad. Now one settlement could see two just a short hike from its doorsteps. What to do?

Pick up and move, Crosby's pioneer citizens decided. The majority to the new G.N. site, carrying along the name of their town. Imperial's residents joined the move as well; its postal service was officially discontinued just nine months after its inception. Finally even the Soo Depot gave up the fight and relocated along with the crowd. The final, successfully merged town — replatted as Crosby Revised — was incorporated in 1911 at a junction of two major railway lines.

Railroad influence spills all over the map of western North Dakota. Northern Pacific directors, officials and their friends scattered names across the west. Among them are Dickinson, honoring railroad land agent Wells Dickinson; Billings County, namesake of the railroad's president at the time of its organization; and Mott, commemorating C.W. Mott, general emigration agent of the N.P.

The Great Northern contributed others . . . Grenora, for example, an acronym of its name, and Williston, a tribute to Jim Hill's friend and stockholder S. Willis James.

The Milwaukee Road christened Bowman, Gascoyne, Griffin and Rhame for various men prominent in its organization, along with Marmarth — a tribute to Margaret Martha

Trainloads of settlers spawned scores of western boomtowns. Cattle brought in for slaughter dominated the streets of Williston in 1911 (opposite page, top), while in Dickinson wagonloads of wool filled the main thoroughfare, Villard, from Sims to First Avenue East. By 1910 Beach (above) supported an impressive array of businesses along its Main Street, apparent evidence that surrounding ranchers and farmers were here to stay.

Fitch, the granddaughter of its president, preserving her childish rendering of her own name.

The towns blessed with a railroad grew while inland settlements struggled to survive. Times were good throughout the second great boom, roughly from 1900 to the end of World War I. New settlers were pouring in as homesteaders or purchasers of public and railroad holdings, their hopes buoyed by good farm prices and a nationwide mania for land.

Town life blossomed as it never had before, and never since. Men and women used to the culture of America's east and midwest established musical societies, literary guilds, opera houses, fresh-painted churches and well-stocked mercantiles. Proud new owners steered Tin Lizzies down broad, bustling Main Streets lined by groceries, dry goods shops, banks, dealers in new power imple-

ments, saloons, drug stores and newspaper offices.

That the wheat and livestock markets would slump and credit be tightened to the point of catastrophe was far from town fathers' minds as they watched their communities prosper and burst into full bloom. It was the honeymoon for newcomers in western North Dakota — the apex of a boom-and-bust cycle that would slip further than they could imagine in the 1920s and 1930s, resurge in the postwar years, and — with the epic of oil and coal — reintroduce wins and losses.

It would weigh its immigrants' resolve. Some would struggle and survive. Many more would leave, wracked by financial ruin, carried away with dust storms barking at their heels. All told, the terrible slow drama would eventually reduce towns by at least two-thirds, testing the people of Dakota's west with its stark abilities to feed them.

By 1909 the town of Alexander — named, like its county, for Boss Alec McKenzie — had sprouted several wood frame buildings along the broad main street typical of western towns. At nearby Arnegard, homesteaders pose in their Sunday finery outside their claim shack; the year is 1913. At right, Robert and Edith Hanson take the evening breeze at their cabin on the Logging Camp Ranch; twining morning glory vines offered a bit of cultivated charm in the setting of harsh natural beauty.

Sentinel Butte, one of the highest points in North Dakota, dominates the small border town that shares its name.

Scoria, the reddish brick baked by burning coal veins from native clay, lends color to ribbon-like badlands roads cutting through the vivid buttes, dull grass and silvery green sagebrush. Badlands tourism was given a boost by construction of Interstate 94, enabling traffic to at last travel safely through the crumpled landscape throughout the year. This section of the highway earned the North Dakota Highway Department a design award for its harmonious integration of roadway and countryside.

Lost Bridge (top), north of Killdeer on Highway 22, was aptly named. Funded and then built on the eve of the Great Depression, it stood alone for more than 25 years after the state ran out of money to construct connecting highways on either side. Parts of Four Bears Bridge (at left) once stood at Elbowoods; that older predecessor was dismantled at the time of Garrison Dam, and incorporated into the new structure bridge at New Town. The famous Long X Bridge on Highway 85 above the North Unit of Roosevelt National Park was first used by cowboys driving herds of cattle across the Little Missouri.

The inky blackness of North Dakota's only railroad tunnel (now unused) frames the Fairview Lift Bridge spanning the Yellowstone. The nearby Snowden Bridge (inset) was used by both trains and motor vehicles, the latter crossing on heavy wooden planks between the rails. Also a lift-span bridge, it once rose to permit steamboats to pass beneath it.

North Dakota's major northwestern city, Williston, has known the frenetic growth of boom times not once but twice — first during the excitement of oil's discovery in the 1950s, and again in the early 1980s when over 150 drilling rigs worked the Williston Basin. Epping's frontier charm survives (above) thanks to artist-historian Elmer Halvorson, who has personally completed much of its restoration.

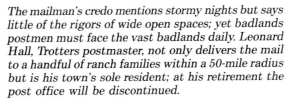

The mailman's credo mentions stormy nights but says little of the rigors of wide open spaces; yet badlands postmen must face the vast badlands daily. Leonard Hall, Trotters postmaster, not only delivers the mail to a handful of ranch families within a 50-mile radius but is his town's sole resident; at his retirement the post office will be discontinued.

Mott postmaster Bob Kammen (above) is an author of several western novels full of blazing guns, cowboys, roundups, badmen and heroes. His latest book incorporates references to Mott's history. The weather-beaten Grassy Butte Post Office (right) is a national historic site, the only sod-and-log postal facility in the nation; it now houses a museum.

Days proceed in quiet peace in western North Dakota. "That Fifi, she sure likes to play. She's a good dog," says Alton Enget (far left) of Epping. On Main Street in Regent (above) the Turbiville sisters, seven-year-old Darlene and Susan, five, ride their bikes on a still summer afternoon. Mike Lutens, owner of Marmarth's Past Time Bar, shares the story of his discovery of dinosaur bones with a young enthusiast. A team of paleontologists spent the summer of 1987 locating and mapping dinosaur remains in the area.

Dickinson lives up to its cow-town reputation each Tuesday and Thursday when area ranchers truck their livestock to two sales rings. Buyers look over about 1,500 head of cattle (top right) at Stockmen's Livestock and hogs at rival Western Livestock Sales (lower right). A motorcycle is employed to drive cattle from ranchers' trucks to pens to await auction in the sales ring.

High school bull riders view the animals they've drawn in Bowman (above), their reactions varying with the size of the beasts' horns. Old-timers in Belfield (top left) play cards and discuss cattle prices, the hay crop and when the next rain might fall. Cowboys still swear the best coffee in Dickinson is at Stockmen's Livestock, where they discuss cattle prices, the hay crop and when the next rain might fall.

A trio of comrades occupy a 90-degree July morning watching traffic and sipping coffee in the shade of Mott's Holiday House. Once the Brown Hotel, it was originally named for the company that founded the Cannonball River city. Leonard Hall of Trotters gets plenty of company including an oilfield worker from Montana, who drops in for a can of soda, chips and the latest news. Carolyn and Jerry Erickson operate their Country Store in Amidon, providing not only groceries but a meeting place and coffee shop.

The shell of Marmarth's old Opera House sits forlorn and neglected, a relic of the days when westbound railroad passengers spent the night and were entertained by traveling theatre troupes. The Mystic Theater, built across the street in 1914, still hosts events like the Shakespeare Festival of 1986. Epping was the first community for a re-energized Chautauqua, a traveling tent show combining entertainment with serious messages; Clay Jenkinson (above) recreates the musings of Meriwether Lewis there on a warm night in July.

89

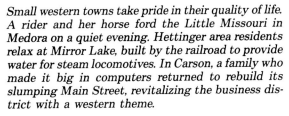

Small western towns take pride in their quality of life. A rider and her horse ford the Little Missouri in Medora on a quiet evening. Hettinger area residents relax at Mirror Lake, built by the railroad to provide water for steam locomotives. In Carson, a family who made it big in computers returned to rebuild its slumping Main Street, revitalizing the business district with a western theme.

Natural resources are the lifeblood of western Dakota, ebbing and flowing with the international markets. New England (above) once shipped more wheat than any other point on the rail line; today a farmers' cooperative owns all five. Families picnic at Scranton on a summer weekend (top left); many residents make their livings mining lignite. The struggle to preserve Golden Valley Medical Center in Beach encapsulates the side effects of erratic markets for oil and farm products. After closing for several years, it reopened in 1987, again serving people of an area hundreds of miles wide.

A log cabin more recently used as a barn offers mute testimony to a knack for "making do," familiar among early settlers like the German-Russian immigrant woman (left). Photographed by the Osborn Studio in 1900, her expression reflects a grim determination to make a new life in North Dakota.

The Immigrants

As the nineteenth century ended and the twentieth began, a motley crew of public and private interests shared a single preoccupation: To sell off the empty lands of western Dakota.

Their motives varied, each blending a modicum of concern for the public welfare with far more specific covert motives. The railroads wanted to fill up the lonely midsections of their transcontinental routes to generate steady, hard-cash traffic. The state of North Dakota wanted solid citizens to swell its population and carry it into a prosperous new era with a broader tax base. The land speculators wanted population, too. . . population to increase demand for the property they held so that it could be sold at values far higher than the bargain prices they's paid.

The Northern Pacific had long advertised its holdings— the "fertile Eden" granted it by the American government—in terms both glowing and only marginally honest. Now, with the arrival of James J. Hill's Great Northern Railway, another clever dreamer joined the wildly optimistic chorus.

Hill imagined the country his rails traversed as an agrarian paradise. Vigorously he promoted his vision of a prosperous, neatly-tended country populated by farm families growing wealthy amidst a thick network of bustling towns similar to those of the old Midwest. . .the sincere unrealistic goal that earned him the title "empire builder." His agents labored to interest dissatisfied men and women in the soil-based riches Hill believed were theirs for the taking.

The young state of North Dakota joined the chorus of hallelujahs celebrating its sparsely-occupied western counties. The 1905 legislature earmarked $20,000 to be used for self-promotion. During the next five years that sum and much more was invested in nearly a million magazines, brochures, maps and circulars.

And a corps of shrewd capitalists joined the campaign. Speculators purchased vast tracts of land from the railroads and then organized land companies to reap the profits. Among them were James C. Young of Minneapolis, who held a million acres in several locations including the vicinity of Dickinson; W.H. Brown and Company of Chicago, with nearly a quarter-million acres south of Richardton; the Western Land Securities Company in Stark County, and the Golden Valley Land and Cattle Company, namesake of that county.

The time was right for future Dakotans to hear their swelling voices. The free lands of the West were nearly gone; farm prices were good, and experts were advising the nation that with its population outstripping food production, farmers would be the wealthy class of the future.

The Homestead Act, which had helped to settle eastern North Dakota, was revised in 1912 to allow individuals to gain title to public land in three (rather than five) years. Too, they could acquire a deed by commuting their claims after only fourteen months' residence. To commute, they paid $1.25 per acre, or $2.50 if their fields were within the railroad land grant.

A torrent of newcomers flooded the western counties between 1900 and the end of World War I. Tens of thousands of men and women stepped off trains in wind-swept barren settings with their children and belongings in tow. Others jounced across the prairie in ox-driven wagons or rattle-trap Fords until they found a likely spot.

Some were farmers from states to the east, either native-born or immigrants who'd arrived years earlier. Though their background in raising crops in a more humid and hospitable climate did not prepare them for the rigors of North Dakota, their enter-

The railroads carried settlement to western Dakota, but land companies played major roles in drawing individuals and families to the new frontier. One of them was the William H. Brown Company headquartered in Mott.

prises did seem to begin with some advantage.

The rest—about half of the new arrivals— had no farming experience at all. Some were caught up in land fever. Some romanticized the farming life. Some were speculating, pure and simple, that real estate prices would rocket as soon as this last American frontier was settled.

For a time, they all seemed right. Generous rains were delivered right on schedule. Farm prices were good. Banks were granting loans to help farmers increase the size of their holdings and modernize with steam tractors and implements. Bumper crops came in, allowing even the least knowledgeable farmer to take pride in his success.

The rosy outlook was sustained until the end of World War I. Then disillusionment set in. The least successful or committed were the first to go, with neighbors buying their land. The process continued steadily until average

farm size was twice what it had begun. At the same time, though, farmers' debt load multiplied. When difficult times arrived in the 1920s, followed by all-out desolation in the 1930s, the character of every rural neighborhood shifted to accommodate the survivors.

Those who'd come farthest were most likely to stay. That tendency distilled the west into a rich cultural brew that still exists today. The ethnic maps of historian William Sherman show polka dots and stripes of other nationalities against two dominant background: Norwegians in northwestern North Dakota, and Germans from Russia across much of the southwest.

As in the rest of North Dakota, immigration followed a distinct pattern.

First came Americans and Canadians with roots in the British Isles, comfortable and familiar with this country's ways. In the west,

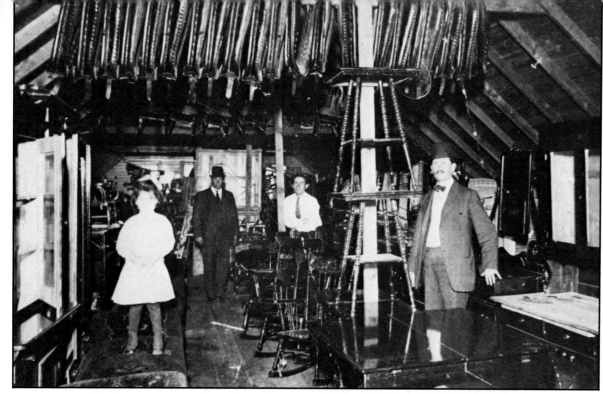

Turn-of-the-century homesteaders at Richardton shopped at Max Marcovitz's general store, packed with a substantial inventory of nearly every essential.

they were not only cowboys and pioneer ranchers, but the founders of towns and among the earliest homesteaders. While many moved on during the perennial trials of drought, grasshoppers, low prices for wheat and beef, and economic travail, their descendants still dominate a broad section of land butting up against the Montana line from Bowman to McKenzie Counties.

Accompanying them were Norwegians and Germans who'd first settled in more densely populated states—Minnesota, Wisconsin, Iowa, Illinois and even eastern North Dakota. They'd begun to learn the language and the customs of the United States, and moved confidently toward the west.

Jim Hill's proselytizing was particularly effective among the Norwegians. To this day they predominate in northwestern North Dakota, the most thoroughly Norse section of the state—one peppered with Danes, Finns and Swedes as well.

Other people came in self-contained colonies, holding their native tongues and folkways close to their hearts. Most prominent among them were the Germans from Russia, whose grandparents and great-grandparents had followed the pioneer trail from Germany to the steppes of Russia. They form a majority in five west river counties, including Grant, Hettinger, Stark, Morton and Mercer. Religious beliefs separated them into two distinct pluralities. Toward the east, they tend to be Protestant; to the west, solidly Catholic.

Other delegations arrived, too, sharing common religious or geographic ties. German-Hungarians took up land east of Dickinson, with Bohemians to the northwest. Ukrainians settled north of Belfield and east of Grassy Butte.

Still other ethnic communities appeared for a few years early in the century. A contingent from Holland located in the South Heart region. Jewish immigrants filed claims near Flasher and Rhame. Syrians or Lebanese, some Moslem and some Christian, settled in Williams and Mountrail Counties. Black homesteaders pioneered south of Alexander, and a group of Japanese took up land in Williams and Mountrail Counties.

The ethnic loyalties of settlement days remained largely intact from the Great Depression until the great elation created by the discovery of oil and natural gas, first in the Tioga area during the 1950s, and then across much of the west in the 1970s. Drilling crews, refineries, pipelines and the industries created to serve the petroleum industry brought significant numbers of new people into sleepy towns that had quietly developed a common history over the past half-century.

For a time these latest of immigrants played a reprise of the early ranching era, when another west-river resource drew newcomers north from Texas and Oklahoma. Familiar Norwegian and German brogues still dominant in the region's town were punctuated by drawls and twangs, sound strangely more foreign than the normal "ja" and "uf da." While four-wheel-drive pickups and semi trucks raised clouds of red scoria dust in back corners of badlands and prairie, settlements of trailers and tract houses swelled local populations and tested civic resources. It resembled a batch of instant prosperity: Just add oil and stir.

Again like the early ranchers, they were only passing through. When the price of petroleum dropped by fifty percent, the immigrants of the 1980s inevitably moved on, just as the cattle barons had a hundred years before when taxation and pioneer pressure raised the ante.

Improving prices of beef and wheat drew others to take the cattle kings' place on smaller ranches and farms. Whether the same may come true of contemporary "cowboys" who ride herd on the wealth of the Williston Basin remains to be seen.

Descendants of Ukrainian immigrants cling to their traditional religion — a devotion evident at Sts. Peter and Paul Church at New Hradec and (opposite) the Catholic school, church and cemetery at Haymarsh. Churches brought pioneer families together for religion, socializing and education, often the only break in their regimen of backbreaking labor.

The Brothers of St. Benedict welcome parishioners and visitors to Assumption Abbey at Richardton, a looming architectural landmark rightly called "The Gem of the Prairie" founded by Abbot Vincent de Paul Wehrle. Its first building, completed in 1900, was used as a church, school and monastery while the Bavarian Romanesque cathedral was being built of Hebron brick. At the time of its first service on Christmas Eve, 1908, it was the largest church building in the state — made even larger by expansion the following year. Monks operated the school continuously until its closure in 1971.

Father James Reilly (above), a priest at the abbey for 57 years, prays over the graves of his parents and sister.

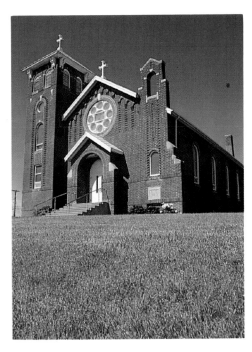

Iron crosses mark the graves of immigrants and their families, a hallmark of German-Russian craftsmanship. Large, distinctive churches mark the horizons of many towns — clockwise from top, Trinity Lutheran in Mott, built of fieldstone; St. Vincent's Catholic Church and School in Mott; St. John's Ukrainian Catholic Church and nearby St. Peter and Paul Orthodox Ukrainian, both of Belfield.

Fewer than a dozen rural one-room schools remain in North Dakota, all but two within the borders of the badlands. Sparse population and enormous distances dictate their small enrollments. But new wealth from oil has enabled even the smallest to be equipped with the latest in technology and teaching aids.

Turn-of-the-century schools were crude but successful in educating the region's young . . . among them a sod school near Zahl, operated from 1903 to 1913; Gamache School in McKenzie County; with six students, and Opperud School, whose ten students posed for a portrait in 1907.

A cable car, not a schoolbus, carries two students and their teacher to Connell School in Billings County. Among its facilities is an apartment for overnight stays in stormy weather. Accompanying teacher Karen Goldsberry is Lar O'Brien (right), county superintendent of schools, who regularly visits each of the five in her district. The end of school year '86-87 was observed with presentation of scholarship trophies to the entire student body — thira grader Julie Goldsberry, and fourth graders Travis Con nell and Nancy Goldsberry — and a potluck dinner and dance in Medora.

102

The bell tower from the old Medora school presides over a new, modern structure made possible by the petroleum extraction tax. Its effects are felt at other schools as well, equipped with up-to-date amenities like the computer used by Richard Romanyshn and Amanda Kadrmas at Snow School, also in Billings County. At Stevenson School (right) in McKenzie County, two students work on composition and spelling. The tiny enrollment has its strengths, among them a great deal of personal attention.

Oil wells were drilled within sight of Williston, a refinery, farms and mobile home courts during the boom years of the early 1980s, when more than 150 rigs were biting into the earth in the Williston Basin. When prices plummeted from $60 to less than $20 a barrel, shock waves rocked the region's economy.

Beneath Their Feet

Western North Dakota's riches come from the earth — not only grasses rooted in its soil and the rain that waters them, but natural resources deep underfoot in the vaults of the Williston Basin.

"A rainfall in India or a hot wind is felt upon the Dakota farm within a few hours," observed famed midwestern journalist William Allen White in 1897. "The wages of the harvester in the Red River Valley are fixed by conditions in the fields of Russia, or Argentina, or in India."

White was describing the business of wheat farming, where the profitability of North Dakota's bountiful grain-growing soils was (and is) determined not on a local, state or national basis, but by the complex interplay of conditions and markets that span the planet.

But his remarks were (and are) just as aptly applied to the other natural resources of western North Dakota — the harvest of lignite coal, petroleum and a dozen other mineral commodities. Like grains and beef, their market price depends not on the difficulty with which they're wrenched from the earth, but on worldwide conditions. Their value rises and falls with largely political events . . . a federally-mandated move toward low-sulfur coals, for example, or a shrewd alliance of petroleum-producing Arabs.

Like wheat, the price of western Dakota's coal and oil is a variable based on factors far out of producers' reach. And like those whose livelihood depends on wheat, workers in North Dakota's energy industry look to worldwide headlines to divine their prosperity or ruin.

A diverse economy has been North Dakota's dream since its earliest days, when wheat became king and tied the state forever to its fluctuating fortunes. Its vast mineral resources were recognized even before statehood as an opportunity to smooth out the erratic twists of an economy based solely on the grain markets. Zealously mapped by the North Dakota Geological Survey and studied by the University of North Dakota's School of Mines, their discovery brought new hope that mining and related kinds of manufacturing would balance out Dakota's agricultural revenues.

History would demonstrate that silver linings do come wrapped in clouds — that dependence on mineral wealth initiates a boom-and-bust cycle that can have devastating effects on dreams of growth and stability.

Lignite coal perhaps ranks third — albeit a distant third — to North Dakota's soil and water as a vast and valued resource. Conservative estimates place the state's unmined reserve at 350 million tons.

Lignite is a young coal, still high in bulk and moisture. Burned for heat, it produces awesome clinkers; its energy is less concentrated than the more familiar anthracite and bituminous grades mined in the eastern United States. Nevertheless, it has long been seen as a resource worthy of development — and one which has drastically altered life in parts of western North Dakota.

Its possibilities were already recognized in territorial days. An 1887 pamphlet entitled *Resources of Dakota* pointed toward western Dakota's ubiquitous deposits as "that inestimable boon, cheap domestic fuel." Farmers and ranchers dug lignite to heat their homes, occasionally peddling wagonloads in town for a dollar or two per ton.

The state's first commercial mining was begun in 1883 east of Dickinson at Lehigh, named for the coal-mining city in Pennsylvania. Purchased by the Pittsburgh

Abundant lignite greeted western North Dakota's first settlers, who mined it to heat their homes. Early underground mines like this one in McKenzie County were small and dangerous.

Coal Company in 1900, the area's sooty veins are still being stripped today for the Royal Oak briquetting plant, employing a process to increase the fuel's effective BTUs developed by the UND School of Mines.

Western North Dakota's early miners burrowed for coal in damp underground corridors, uncomfortable and dangerous. The deep mines' heyday extended from 1902 to 1919, though the last of the breed, the Square Deal Coal Mine of Williams County, carried on until 1950.

The break for daylight came near Kincaid in Burke County where two lignite firms, Whittier Coal Company and Truax Brothers, established the first effective strip mines. Horsedrawn scrapers were first used to strip the overburden from seams, then to dredge up coal which other teams hauled away in dump

wagons. In 1919 they replaced animals with a steam shovel and steam locomotive to haul narrow-gauge pit cars to the tipple.

Today the bulk of North Dakota's lignite industry is centered in Mercer, Oliver and Dunn Counties along with electrical generating plants and the nation's first coal gasification plant. That controversial billion-dollar facility was considered experimental in the 1970s. Yet it was foreseen a century before in the brochure *Resources of Dakota*, which noted that lignite had "gas-making qualities superior to almost any fuel found on the continent."

Other companies continue to strip-mine seams of coal in Burke and Bowman Counties, where Scranton owes its name to another Pennsylvania mining town. While the lignite's low sulfur content makes it desirable

On July 20, 1951, the cries of "Oil!" rung throughout the Williston Basin from the site of the Clarence Iverson test well near Tioga. Today North Dakota ranks ninth in U.S. petroleum production.

for smokestack industries striving to meet air quality standards, its bulk leads to relatively high transportation costs. Nevertheless, all but endless trains of open cars loaded with the powdery black coal continue to wind their way eastward to some urban electrical plants.

Several other minerals are interwoven with Dakota's seams of Coal. Leonardite, partially-oxidized brown lignite, is used commercially in the oil industry, in water treatment and as a coloring agent in paints and stain; some three-quarters of the nation's Vandyke brown pigment was created millions of years ago in the state's prehistoric swamps. The substance owes its name to the first director of the state geological survey, A.G. Leonard.

More familiar is uranium, the radioactive raw material of the atomic age. Most of America's supply is milled from uranium-bearing sandstones in Colorado and surrounding states. In Billings County, however, ore-grade deposits were discovered in 1955 amidst lignite beds, where organic materials had absorbed it from groundwater.

Raw ore was first mined in the area between Belfield and Amidon in 1956. Milling methods used to refine uranium from more common sandstone proved inefficient with western Dakota's ores. During the mid-1960s an alternative was developed, with the uraniferous lignite burned to yield ashes, which were then shipped on for further refining.

But richer deposits elsewhere made the refining of North Dakota's uranium economically unfeasible, even though another byproduct of the process, molybdenum, is in increasing demand for use in steel alloys. Attempts to cash in on the ores were set aside.

Geologists anticipated the discovery of oil in the Williston Basin long before the Amerada Petroleum Corporation's drilling rigs struck the jackpot near Tioga in 1951.

Conditions were right. Deep beneath the horizon, the sunken saucer of granite crust contains the wealth of half a billion years of invested time - an energy-rich black soup of primordial jungle foliage and dinosaur bones, brewed beneath successive layers of rock and silt.

Natural gas wells in Williams County date back to the early years of the century. In 1929 the first commercial well was drilled in Bowman County; that and dozens of succeeding wells were tied into a pipeline to supply customers of Montana-Dakota Utilities.

Oil was more elusive. The first drilling rigs bit into the basin in 1919 two miles east of Williston. The hole was plugged at a depth of just over 2,000 feet, its investors unaware that deposits lay more than a mile further down.

Dozens of other wells date from the 1920s into the postwar years — some of them drawing close, but all coming up dry. One unsuccessful 1938 attempt was abandoned just three-quarters of a mile from a later well still pumping today. Yet wildcatters and major companies alike continued to test the depths.

Their persistence was repaid on July 20, 1951, by the well eight miles south of Tioga which Amerada designated as Clarence Iverson No. 1. There, more than two miles beneath the ground, they finally struck black gold.

While newspapers trumpeted the triumph and Tioga blossomed into a boom town, new discoveries spread the attention far across the now-golden Williston Basin. Two months after the first discovery, Amerada logged another win at H.O. Bakken No. 1 a dozen miles away. Others successfully probed the field in subsequent test drillings.

In 1953 wells in Bottineau County came in at shallow depths. That same year brought discoveries west of Dickinson near Fryburg and to the south. Flaxton marked the first well in the fields of Burke and Divide Coun-

Working the oil fields is dirty and dangerous business. Nevertheless petroleum generally coexists well with the high plains' principal industry, agriculture. After drilling is completed the farmer can mow his crop in peace while pumpjacks coax the black gold to the surface and into the pipeline.

ty in 1956. Sixteen years later, drilling rigs in McKenzie County came in with petroleum from an unusually turbulent geologic zone called the Red Wing Creek Structure — believed to have been scrambled by a collision with a meteorite.

Exciting as they were, the Williston Basin's oil deposits shared some disadvantages. They were more expensive to unearth, lying far deeper than the deposits of Texas and Oklahoma, and thus were more expensive to bring to the surface. Too, they were located in a corner of the nation remote from existing refineries. Standard Oil solved part of the problem by building refineries in Mandan and Williston. Pipelines provided another answer, carrying crude oil and refined products eastward to energy-hungry markets.

The excitement of the western North Dakota oil patch had subsided to a far calmer fact of life when, in 1973, the organization of Petroleum Exporting Countries sent the price

of imported oil skyrocketing. Shocked Americans watched the price of heating oil quadruple and gasoline reach the unheard-of level of $1.50 per gallon or more. They recoiled from their casual dependence on distant Arabian states and turned instead to their own distant long-shelved riches.

Suddenly western North Dakota's deep, deep wells took on new significance. Drilling crews moved across tinder-dry pastures and scaled the badlands' lumpy terrain. Heavy equipment pounded new scoria-orange byways. Pumping stations launched their interminable bobbing, adding odd grasshopper-like profiles to a horizon lately dotted by nothing more than buttes and the occasional mute threshing machine.

Prosperity climbed to feverish heights as headlines about OPEC dominated the 1970s. In a fragile land where water only trickled, money flowed.

When the crash came ten years later, the flood evaporated on the wind.

The bloom wore off the boomtowns almost before the next dawn. Dickinson and Williston staggered from the departure of the freespending cowboys of the oil patch and the industries that had grown up to serve their needs. Some smaller towns were all but demolished; massive civic investments in streets and utilities intended to accommodate mushrooming populations instead toppled into ruin as the tumbleweeds prevailed.

When oil prices recover, as they surely will, America will remember the remote petroleum reserves that underline a timeless subterranean basin beneath hardworking farmers' and ranchers' feet. Until then, the relentless lesson North Dakotans have learned time and again will echo along the state's western margin: Prosperity is not to be won from this land, but only purchased at a steep price.

The old Binek Coal Mine marks the site of the venerable lignite field east of Dickinson. Today strip-mined lignite is turned to charcoal briquettes for backyard gourmets at the Royal Oak plant. At Gascoyne, American Colloid operates its similar plant across Highway 12 from a North American Coal Company mine.

Clockwise from right, a pump jack neighboring Roosevelt National Park brings up North Dakota crude, piped to a gas processing plant in the Fryburg Oil Field. Signal Oil's processing plant at Tioga was one of the state's first. After drills locate a producing well, the workover rig transforms it to a producing well. Drill pipe marks the site of another exploration.

A lone bison bull stands in the autumn solitude of the badlands (left). Medora's Rough Riders Hotel (above) was faithfully restored to preserve its century-old character.

Wish You Were Here!

Today hospitality is the lifeblood of the badlands.

When the well-traveled think of North Dakota, their first impression is one of sagebrush, buttes and buffalo—elements of the wilderness that still prevails. Thanks to Theodore Roosevelt and a host of impassioned local advocates, the country that he loved has been preserved in the national park that bears his name and in other tracts protected by state and federal mandate.

Slip away from the paved roads that carry tourists through the unearthly sunken realm, and you can still experience this wild land as he knew it more than a hundred years ago. The whisper of the Little Missouri River, of cottonwoods and birdsong, can be heard free from the persistent bass rhythm of cars and soprano cackle of youngsters playing volleyball in distant campgrounds.

Throughout much of the eight-thousand-square-mile landscape, the primitive hand of its sculptor is still at work. The Little Missouri River, sluggish now and brown with suspended mud, still eats away at the feet of sandstone cliffs and concretions. The wind still scours the face of buttes and sends tumbleweeds bouncing into the wooded draws.

Hell with the fires out? Sully was wrong. The fires still burn beneath the hooves of antelope and hikers' Adidas. Touched off by lightning or prairie fire, they feed on crumbling veins of lignite deep in the earth, sending rivulets of smoke into the chilly air of dawn to remind the satisfied that the earth's forces, once provoked, cannot be banked to let mortals rest easy.

Roosevelt recognized an ironically fragile balance when he first came to test himself against the badlands' splendid power. He knew the buffalo which he hunted with great zest were certainly doomed. He knew the nation's appetite for gobbling up its natural resources. He knew that the free-spirited cat-

113

tlemen's era would only be an interval, and guessed that his fellow citizens' drive for profit and power could undo what had been a planet's lifetime in the building.

When he assumed the presidency after William McKinley's assassination in 1901, he carried along the ethic of conservation along with his full slate of progressive priorities. He vastly accelerated the pace of acquiring wilderness lands for public ownership, laying the foundations for the National Park Service that would someday protect his own wild paradise in his name. (In fact, he did acquire add a tract of Little Missouri bottomland twenty miles south of Medora to the inventory of national forests, though it was subsequently dropped.)

But that would come much later. Though the idea of preserving the badlands in general and his ranch sites in particular came up in local conversation during his terms as the twenty-sixth American president, not until 1921 did it receive official blessing. That year the North Dakota Legislature passed a resolution instructing the state's congressional delegation to "use all honorable means to make the proposed Roosevelt Park a reality."

Statewide efforts to preserve the badlands had begun in 1917 with a resolution calling upon Congress to consider a national park in the Killdeer Mountains. The North Dakota delegation did introduce a bill to that effect in 1919; it failed. But that initiative provided a precedent for much more ambitious action.

Carl B. Olsen, a state representative and proprietor of the Peaceful Valley Ranch, was trail boss on the state's campaign to set aside a grand park in Roosevelt's honor. He introduced the badlands firsthand to delegations of federal and state officials, newspapermen, movie promoters and railroad functionaries in 1923 and 1924. He shepherded them on horseback through the badlands' winding trails, opening their eyes to the stark beauties of nature. . . and not indicentally, creating among the tenderfeet a sharp new apprecia-

Early dudes and sightseers based at Peaceful Valley Ranch probed the rumpled scenery from horseback and stagecoach. Carl B. Olsen, an early operator of the ranch (now within Roosevelt Park) was instrumental in the early movement to preserve the area as a national park.

tion of cowboys who spent their whole lives in the saddle atop a headstrong horse.

Many of those converts joined him in forming the Theodore Roosevelt Memorial National Park Association in August, 1924. They proposed a park extending one hundred fifty miles from north to south and forty from east to west, including not only the badlands from Marmarth to Grassy Butte as well as the Killdeer Mountain. The state engineer prepared a detailed map of the area, showing each parcel of private land along with public and railroad holdings.

The effort to solicit support in Washington, D.C., met with a fair degree of resistance. The Department of Agriculture mounted a survey of the area, concluding that it included "much of scenic charm and of scientific interest and value. . . The general area is of comparatively little economic importance in the ordinary sense . . .but of high potential value for recreation and game preserve purposes." Federal recommendations focused on a sort of dude

ranch offering living history lessons in old-style cattle ranching.

They also urged North Dakota to take on the project itself as a state park—something that the Legislature, caught in the grim local economic vise of the 1920s, could not do. The 1929 Legislature did, however, approve a proposal to contribute school lands to the federal government if a park were to be established.

In 1932 the director of the National Park Service conducted an aerial tour of the proposed parklands. He suggested plans to scaled down to a national monument, adding, "The park as originally planned is too big."

Acquiring privately-owned land was a central obstacle to the proposal. That changed, though, as the depression deepened and nearly rainless years took their toll on badlands ranchers and farmers. Many gave up their land and moved away. Land prices dropped by half, and the great majority of those who farmed the dusty lands of the west were forced to go on federal relief programs.

Still-echoing advice to "see North Dakota first" was heeded by early badlands tourists, even those — like Robert and Edith Hanson of Amidon and sons James and Donald — who spent their lives amidst pastel buttes and shadowed gullies.

The Rural Resettlement Administration bought up vast tracts of submarginal land for an average of two dollars an acre, ending up with two areas to be used as recreation demonstration projects. The Civilian Conservation Corps, under sponsorship of the North Dakota Historical Society, located camps near them at Medora and Watford City, employing hundreds of struggling men from the region's farms and towns to lay out camping sites, picnic grounds and hiking trails. Other alphabet agencies of the New Deal followed suit in trying to sustain hard-hit Dakotans through public works, including the Federal Emergency Relief Administration and the Works Progress Administration.

At the same time, broad social changes were bringing the badlands far closer to the American mainstream. Improved highways and better cars were scaling down the distance. Tourism was coming to be recognized as a sources of economic stability and growth. A growing population suggested the need for more recreation and park lands.

The badlands park site became a wildlife refuge briefly in 1946. But Congressman William Lemke lobbied unceasingly for North Dakota's preferred use, a national park. He introduced a bill to that effect encompassing the present southern unit of the park. It passed both houses but was vetoed by Harry Truman at the urging of National Park Service officials.

Lemke resumed the fight in 1947, adding the Elkhorn Ranch to his bill and relenting to accept the designation suggested by the still-reluctant Park Service, Theodore Roosevelt National Memorial Park. Once again his measure passed, and this time the president signed it. The north unit was added in 1948.

On June 4, 1949, a crowd estimated at from twenty to forty thousand crowded the sides of the natural amphitheatre of Painted Canyon to witness the dedication of the nation's first and only national memorial park. It climaxed twenty-eight years of organized effort by North Dakotans, and represented a final compromise—albeit a minor one—in their dream for a national park to take its place among the magnificent treasures of the west.

That word, **memorial,** came to sting a bit, seemingly sentencing the park in Roosevelt's honor to perennial runner-up status. Tourism promoters repeatedly petitioned Congress for true national park status, free and clear. On Nov. 10, 1978, they had their wish. Jimmy Carter at last signed a bill dropping the offending eight-letter word from the park's official name and designating almost half of its thirty thousand acres a national wilderness area.

Preserving the wilderness is one thing, outfitting it for guests another.

Tourists willingly spend their days wandering among its rocky pillars and buttes, riding over precipitous horsepaths or viewing the feral landscape from an air-conditioned automobile. For their nights they demand, at minimum, a hearty steak, a hot shower and a comfortably pillowed bed.

In Yellowstone and elsewhere the National Park Service plays the host, developing guest accommodations at public expense. In Theodore Roosevelt National Park that was not meant to be, thanks to the commitment of businessman Harold Schafer.

Schafer, a North Dakota industrialist who made his fortune selling household products, brought a native's love of the wild western country to the sleepy cowboy village of Medora. He fell in love with the sagas of its past, of the romantic Marquis and Marquise de Mores and the greenhorn intellectual whom the badlands raised to manhood. And he recognized that, if those legends were to be shared with an America desperate for heroes, the public would need a local place to eat and sleep.

His involvement with the town of Medora began with a simple philanthropic act. He purchased the crumbling Rough Rider Hotel and offered it to the State Historical Society. The society, though, had no funds to restore the historic building. Instead, director Russell Reid remanded it to Schafer's care. . . and the impetuous businessman took it on himself in 1965.

Guests who stayed in its history-steeped rooms needed to eat, to entertain their children, to taste more of the place's authentic legendry. Gradually the Gold Seal Company developed more twentieth-century amenities and entertainments.

Doc Hubbard, an aficionado and authority on Indian and cowboy life, established his Indian and Wildlife Museum to tell the badlands' story through the remnants of its past. The Burning Hills Amphitheatre southwest of town came to life with nightly variety programs blending lively song and dance with dollops of true western flavor.

Campsites, restaurants and a comfortable sprawling motel took root, along with public facilities (a swimming pool, a convention center) and shops to provision tourist families with necessities, from cookout staples to western souvenirs. Coupled with nationwide promotion and Americans' growing lust to savor the great epics of their past, Medora has taken its place as the natural complement to the wilderness of the parklands.

While Medora and Theodore Roosevelt National Park are the best-known destinations along North Dakota's western margin, they're by no means its sole attractions.

A variety of historical and natural sites are strung out, connect-the-dots fashion, from north to south along the Montana border.

The restoration of Fort Union promises a much-needed passage back in time to the days when it was the most famous spot on the upper Missouri. Along with Fort Buford a few miles to the east, the federally-funded program introduces the lore of Indians and fur traders who negotiated their deals near the junction of the Yellowstone and Missouri Rivers.

Public lands surround Lake Sakakawea, the giant reservoir of the Missouri River which covers many sites significant in those days. Development of its recreational potential has brought fishermen by the thousands, skimming the lake on the path of lunker walleyes.

Lewis and Clark State Park near Williston and Fort Stevenson State Park near Garrison provide campsites for recreational vehicles and launch ramps for motorboats, with other facilities provided around the lake by the U.S. Corps of Engineers and private resort developers.

Little Missouri State Park offers a fully primitive alternative near the site of the old Long X Ranch. Its inner reaches are open only to hikers, tent campers and trail-riders. Here the violent churning landscape meets the mirror-calm lakeshore.

Their tryst is marked by skeleton trees and rocky rubble, physical testimony that change is inevitable in this evolving land. That principle is displayed throughout the region. . .

above the still-red embers at the burning coal vein near Amidon, with its twisted junipers and ponderosa pine. . .

in the tall flat buttes that abruptly break the rolling prairie. . .

in marine fossils crumbling near the roots of prickly pear and sage. . .

in the comical nodding oil wells pumping up the legacy of dinosaurs, primeval swamps and war soupy seas.

This is a lonely land that time has not forgotten. It is not a monument to the past, a past that holds back the future. It is a stark reminder that change can never be denied, and that change, despite the pain, brings worlds of beauty.

When young Theodore Roosevelt arrived to hunt in the badlands, the only brand of civilization encountered in Medora was pool hall life at the Rough Riders Hotel.

Medora 1906

Medora was quiet by the turn of the century. A friend remarked to Roosevelt that it was about to blow away, leaving only a fence post and a hole in the ground. "You're lucky to have the hole," the future president replied.

The first of Medora's deteriorating landmarks to be restored were the Rough Riders Hotel and Joe Ferris Store, both completed in 1965 through the philanthropy of North Dakota industrialist Harold Schafer.

The North Unit of Theodore Roosevelt National Park offers a spectacular view of a Little Missouri oxbow. With its far higher elevation, the remote area's buttes appear more rugged than more familiar sights in the South Unit. Bison and Texas longhorn cattle roam the cottonwoods of the bottoms.

118

The badlands and the Little Missouri River, its principal sculptor, accommodate those wistful for the privacy of a primitive wilderness. Highways carry visitors to the brink of the stony wonderland, but the best way to discover its secrets is to plunge in afoot, on horseback or in a canoe.

The badlands' palette changes with the seasons. Wild horses forage in the usually-scant snow cover of deep winter. Pink scoria peaks are accented by the deep greens and greys of summer. Autumn rushes past in a few days of red and golden splendor, rivaling the fiery year-round sunsets and the fireworks of spring thunderstorms that quickly invest their precious moisture.

Everchanging light gives the badlands an almost mystical appeal. Glimpse a milling herd of horses stirring the dust at sunset. Ponder the vast brushstrokes of Painted Canyon. The Old West drama of heroes and badmen haunts these vistas — a ghost embraced by time.

North Dakota businessman Harold Schafer has guided development of Medora into one of the Great Plains' leading tourist attractions. A aficionado of western Americana and of Theodore Roosevelt, he has directed restoration of several buildings and creation of attractions for family-style vacations. Schafer and wife Sheila appeared in a Fourth of July parade driving an automotive version of Glass Wax, the product he made famous. After the sale of the Gold Seal Company in 1986, Schafer assigned management of the Medora operation to the Theodore Roosevelt Medora Foundation, whose board of directors includes a descendant of the one-time rancher along with prominent North Dakotans.

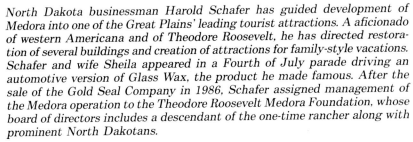

The Medora Musical has entertained countless families on summer nights since 1962, carrying out its folksy patriotic themes in song and dance to as many as 2,000 guests per night. A new cast of aspiring young performers, many of them from North Dakota and neighboring states, joins the roster each spring. They balance nights in the spotlight with days spent industriously waiting tables and clerking in Medora businesses. Each harbors a dream of stardom to rival alumnus Tom Netherton, discovered on stage by Lawrence Welk.

The great American sport of rodeo highlights the western Dakota summer. Among the biggest is the Champions Ride, a date on the Professional Rodeo Cowboys Association circuit held at Home on the Range for Boys, a rehabilitation program for teens. Western North Dakotans number among the sport's great heroes — most recently, top bronc rider Brad Gjermundson of Marshall. Most dangerous of all is bull riding, where rodeo clowns play a serious role in the arena in addition to amusing the crowds.

Sunset against the harsh badlands horizon set the scene for Roughrider Country, North Dakota's most famous and successful tourism promotion campaign. Selling North Dakota's western image has become a good business for the hospitality industry.

Dodge borrowed the badlands cowboy's reputation for tough dependability with its introduction of the Dodge Dakota pickup. Classic western scenes provided authenticity as well as atmosphere — a barbecue, fancy roping and riding, and deft driving along scoria roads where vertical occasionally dominates the horizon.

Russ Hanson, Nancy Edmonds Hanson, Sheldon Green

Nancy Edmonds Hanson is a frequent contributor to *North Dakota Horizons* and other regional and national magazines, and is director of public relations with Hetland Ltd. of Fargo. Raised in Hillsboro and Streeter, she has written two national bestselling guides for freelance writers; produced a weekly news program for statewide public television; edited a variety of periodicals, and founded Prairie House, a publisher of regional books. The former Fargo *Forum* reporter and assistant state travel director attended Concordia College and graduated from Moorhead State University in 1971.

Sheldon Green is the editor of *North Dakota Horizons* Magazine. A native of Hatton, he graduated from the University of North Dakota in 1971. He was editor of the Hazen Star for ten years during the time of coal conversion development in western North Dakota. Green has also worked for daily newspapers in Idaho and Green Bay, Wisconsin, where he developed and edited a weekend magazine supplement. His writing, photography and design have won several awards and his work has appeared in national publications. He lives with his wife and family in Bismarck.

Russ Hanson is director of photography with Hetland Ltd. of Fargo. Formerly chairman of Bismarck Junior College's graphic arts department, the Mandan native has contributed photographs to a long list of state, regional and national books and periodicals, from *North Dakota Horizons* to *Midwest Living* to National Geographic Books. He is a 1968 graduate of BJC and earned his degree in photography and cinematography from Southern Illinois University in 1970. He, his wife Nancy and their daughter Patti live in Fargo-Moorhead.

Bibliography

American Guide Series. *North Dakota, A Guide to the Northern Prairie State.* New York: Oxford University Press, 1939; second edition, 1950.

Bluemle, John P. *Face of North Dakota: The Geological Story.* Grand Forks ND: North Dakota Geological Survey, Educational Series 11.

Clark, Champ. *The Badlands.* New York: Time-Life Books, 1974.

Eidem, R.J., and Goodman, L.R. *The Atlas of North Dakota.* Fargo ND: North Dakota Studies Inc., 1976.

Innis, Ben. *Sagas of the Smoky Water.* Williston ND: Centennial Press, 1985.

Jelliff, Theodore B. *North Dakota: A Living Legacy.* Fargo ND: K&K Publishers, 1983.

Leifur, Conrad W. *Our State North Dakota.* New York: American Book Company, 1942; revised 1945 and 1953.

Morris, Edmund. *The Rise of Theodore Roosevelt.* New York: Coward, McCann and Geoghegan Inc., 1979.

Palmer, Bertha Rachael. *Beauty Spots of North Dakota.* Bostom MA: The Gorham Press, 1928.

Robinson, Elwyn B. *History of North Dakota.* Lincoln NE: University of Nebraska Press, 1966.

Roosevelt, Theodore. *Ranch Life in the Far West.* Flagstaff AZ: Northland Press, 1968; reprinted from *Century* Magazine, 1988.

Sherman, William C. *Prairie Mosaic, An Ethnic Atlas of Rural North Dakota.* Fargo ND: Institute for Regional Studies, 1983.

Tweton, D. Jerome. *The Marquis de Mores: Dakota Capitalist, French Nationalist.* Fargo ND: Institute for Regional Studies, 1972.

Vestal, Stanley. *The Missouri.* New York: Holt, Rinehart and Winston, 1945; reprinted by University of Nebraska press, 1964.

Wemett, William Marks. *The Story of the Flickertail State.* Valley City ND: By the author, 1923.

White, Helen McCann. *Ho! For the Gold Fields.* St. Paul MN: Minnesota Historical Society Press, 1966.

Wilkins, Robert P. and Wilkins, Wynona Huchette. *North Dakota, A Bicentennial History.* New York: W.W. Norton and Company, in association with American Association for State and Local History, 1977.

Williams, Mary Ann Barnes. *Origins of North Dakota Place Names.* Bismarck ND: By the author, 1966; reprinted by McLean County Historical Society, 1973.

Acknowledgements

*The board of directors and staff of the Greater North Dakota Association, without whose approval and support this project would not be possible.

*The North Dakota Bankers Association, whose early endorsement helped launch this once-in-a-hundred-years book series.

*North Dakota Horizons Magazine, in which some of these photographs originally appeared.

*Larry Brown of Fargo, owner of the Osborn Collection of classic western photographs, and photocolorist Fran Thune of Moorhead.

*The family of Robert and Edith Hanson, whose love of photography has been handed down across the generations, and whose legacy includes many of the historic photos in this book.

*Todd Strand and the photo archives, State Historical Society of North Dakota.

*Additional photographs by Nancy Edmonds Hanson, Ken Jorgenson and Tim Kjos.

*Steve Gorman, for his encouragement.

Library of Congress Cataloging-in-Publication Data

Hanson, Nancy Edmonds, 1949-
    Sagebrush, buttes, and buffalo.

    (North Dakota centennial series; v. 4)
    Bibliography: p.
    1. North Dakota — History, Local. 2. North Dakota — Social life and customs. 3. North Dakota — Description and travel — Views. I. Title. II. Series.
    F636.H36   1988   978.4   87-24531
    ISBN 0-911007-08-3

North Dakota Centennial Book Series

'CROSS THE WIDE MISSOURI

BISMARCK AND THE WEST RIVER COUNTRY

North Dakota Centennial Series
Volume One

SAGEBRUSH, BUTTES AND BUFFALO

WILLISTON, DICKINSON AND THE BADLANDS

North Dakota Centennial Series
Volume Four

BREAD BASKET OF THE WORLD

FARGO, GRAND FORKS AND THE RED RIVER VALLEY

North Dakota Centennial Series
Volume Two

HEART OF THE PRAIRIE

MINOT, JAMESTOWN, VALLEY CITY AND DEVILS LAKE

North Dakota Centennial Series
Volume Three

This informative and visually graphic series of books honors North Dakota's first 100 years . . . each volume contains 128-pages, each with over 200 crisp color photographs with an easy-reading text that provides an informative and entertaining mix of North Dakota history, anecdotes, tall tales and frontier stories.

These softbound books form an exciting, contemporary tour of North Dakota that will give you an intimate knowledge of our first 100 years.

Each volume traces the fascinating history of a specific multi-county region of our state . . . and for the first time shows our high quality of life in present day North Dakota. This series forms an authoritative and comprehensive look at our great state.

A new volume will be released every year through the centennial year of 1989.

Volume One: *'Cross the Wide Missouri.* Over 230 color photographs help trace the development of the counties that border the historic Missouri River, from Garrison Dam to Lake Oahe and the days of Custer, steamboats and railroad building.

Volume Two: *Bread Basket of the World.* This is one of the few books available that chronicles the agricultural wealth of the Red River Valley. With over 300 vivid color photos, this volume explores the small towns, the major cities and the diversity of farming that makes this the richest agricultural region in the world.

Volume Three: *Heart of the Prairie.* Prairie potholes teeming with wildlife, scenic rivers, hills and woodlands, makes this region one of the most varied in North Dakota. Over 200 fresh color photos take you to some of our most scenic locations.

Volume Four: *Sagebrush, Buttes and Buffalo.* Perhaps the most eagerly awaited volume of the series, this magnificent edition explores the Badlands . . . the colorful characters of the past, the rugged beauty of the hills carved from fire and water . . . and the persistent ranchers and oilmen who labor daily in this spectacular region. With over 200 vivid color photographs from every season, this volume displays the Badlands as they've never been seen before.

872002   386   386007